How to Succeed as an Officer in Today's U.S. Army

Leroy Sharpe, Jr.

(LTC, U.S. Army Retired)

ISBN Number: 978-1-57087-814-5

Library of Congress Control Number 2013911181

Professional Press
Chapel Hill, NC 27515-4371

Manufactured in the United States of America
13 14 15 16 17   10 9 8 7 6 5 4 3 2 1

Dedication

This book is dedicated to my deceased parents (Mattrude P. Sharpe and Leroy Sharpe, Sr.) for their love and unwavering support throughout my life. Their words of encouragement and push for tenacity will forever ring in my ears. I will always appreciate all that they have done.

Table of Contents

Foreword by
Lorenzo Riddick (LTC, U.S. Army Retired)

L eroy Sharpe, Jr. (LTC, U.S. Army Retired) wrote this book to help educate, mentor and motivate our next generation of leaders considering joining the military and becoming an U.S. Army Officer. Whether it is JROTC, ROTC, Army Reserve or Active Duty Military, the rich history, lessons, and advice presented in this book will help guide future and current Military Army Officers along the road to success.

Education—You will receive a lesson in African-American Military History: For more than two hundred years, African-Americans have participated in every conflict in United States history. This includes Crispus Attucks' heroic actions during the Revolutionary War, the 54th Massachusetts Infantry's support during the Civil War, the Buffalo Soldiers' participation in the Indian Campaigns, the 369th Regiment and the French *Croix de Guerre* contributions during World War I, the Tuskegee Airmen during World War II, and the countless contributions of thousands of African-Americans during the Korean War, Vietnam War, Desert Shield/ Desert Storm and OEF/OIF campaigns. This book does an amazing job of summarizing these major events while highlighting the contributions of African-American men and women in the U.S. Army.

History of African-American Officers in the U.S. Army: This chapter is complete with profiles of African-Americans who met challenges head-on. They seized their opportunities to make a difference. They showed that African Americans possessed the ability to serve in the capacity of General Officer. These are individuals who helped elevate African-Americans in the armed forces to a much higher place in history. LTC (Ret'd) Leroy Sharpe, Jr. provides you with a detailed, uncensored autobiography, from birth through military retirement, complete with many lessons learned along the way. In addition, he provides timely and accurate advice for the next generation of military officers, to include information on how to become an U.S. Army Officer through one of four commissioning programs: the United States Military Academy, the Army Reserve Officers' Training Corps (ROTC), the Officer Candidate School (OCS), or direct appointment. Throughout his career, LTC (Ret'd) Sharpe has constantly displayed a caring personal leadership style that brought out the best in everyone who worked with him. That caring spirit is on display throughout this entire book.

Conclusion: Regardless of your race and gender, understanding your history helps you prepare for the future. Each generation benefits from the opportunity to surpass the generation preceding it, in part because it stands on the shoulders of its predecessors. The more you can learn from the previous generation, the better your chances are at exceeding all expectations. The purpose of this book is to prepare our next generation of Army Officers for success by exposing them to much of the rich untold history of the U.S. Army. This is enhanced by providing the reader with the real-world autobiography of the author along with lessons learned and advice for our next generation of Army Officers.

Part I
Introduction

IT COULDN'T BE DONE

Somebody said that it couldn't be done,
But he with a chuckle replied
That "maybe it couldn't," but he would be one
Who wouldn't say so till he'd tried.
So he buckled right in with the trace of a grin
On his face. If he worried he hid it.
He started to sing as he tackled the thing
That couldn't be done, and he did it.
Somebody scoffed: "Oh, you'll never do that;
At least no one ever has done it";
But he took off his coat and he took off his hat,
And the first thing we knew he'd begun it.
With a lift of his chin and a bit of a grin,
Without any doubting or quiddit,
He started to sing as he tackled the thing
That couldn't be done, and he did it.
There are thousands to tell you it cannot be done,
There are thousands to prophesy failure;
There are thousands to point out to you, one by one,
The dangers that wait to assail you.
But just buckle in with a bit of a grin,
Just take off your coat and go to it;
Just start to sing as you tackle the thing
That "cannot be done," and you'll do it."

—By Edgar A. Guest

1

This poem is a constant reminder of the naysayers who constantly doubted me; the ones who did not think that a young black kid out of the 'hood in Portsmouth, Virginia could go off to college, major in Architectural Engineering, get commissioned as an Engineer Officer in the U.S. Army Corps of Engineers, and have a successful career in the U.S. Military. This poem and my naysayers are what motivated me go the extra mile, even when I sometimes felt like giving up. They are what fueled me when I had to stay up all night to complete an Architectural Engineer design project due the next morning. They motivated me on those nights when I was pledging Omega Psi Phi and didn't know what day it was or even where I was at. They fueled me on those nights in Iraq when I was sitting in my foxhole trying to protect myself from the mortars and rounds that bombarded out base camp on a nightly basis. I wrote this book to help educate, mentor, and motivate our next generation of leaders considering joining the military and becoming an officer. Whether it is JROTC, ROTC, Army Reserve or Active Duty Military, the rich history, lessons, and advice presented in this book will help guide any future Military Army Officer through the ups and downs of military life. I've learned many lessons that guided me through the military and life in general. Some were hard lessons brought on by my mistakes; others were inspired by my leaders. Some lessons evolved over the years; others came in a single emotional event. In every case, they became my guiding principles. What follows are a few that may be of use to you.

My name is Leroy Sharpe, Jr. and I am a 47-year-old recent retiree from the U.S. Army Corps of Engineers. My wife, Sonja, and I reside in Chesapeake, Virginia. My father, Leroy Sharpe, Sr., was born September 3, 1933 in Wilson County, NC. He was the second youngest out of five brothers and two sisters to the late Roman and Mattie Bynum Sharpe. He learned the meaning of hard work at an early age. He grew up picking tobacco in the North Carolina tobacco fields. He graduated from Fike High School and joined the U.S. Army. He served thirteen years as a U. S. paratrooper, spending most of his career at Fort Bragg, NC (Home of the Airborne!). He retired on a medical discharge after multiple knee and back injuries. He then moved to Virginia and worked at the Norfolk Naval Shipyard, followed by the U.S. Post Office, before retiring a second time and starting his own furniture upholstery business in Portsmouth, Va. He graduated from Norfolk State College with an Associate's degree in upholstery. His civic memberships include the U.S. Postal Association, Veterans of Foreign Wars (VFW), and the American Legion. He was a member of the Masonic Lodge, Mt.

Gilead Lodge # 102, PHA, and the Mighty O'Jays Social Club. He was a faithful member of the Male and Combined Usher Boards at the New First Baptist Church Taylorsville in Portsmouth. He passed away May 13, 2007 after a long bout with lung cancer. My mother, Mattrude Person Sharpe, was born January 27, 1934 in Branchville, Va. She too was the second youngest (knee-baby) of three brothers and two sisters. She worked on the farm before and after school while growing up in the country. Her parents made sure that she got her education. She was the first in her family to go to college, earning a bachelor's degree in Early Childhood Education from Virginia State College (now University) in Petersburg, Va. She loved children and taught school for over 25 years before having a nervous breakdown. She never fully recovered but eventually returned to the classroom, mostly as a substitute teacher. She was a Sunday School Teacher, Vacation Bible School Teacher, and Senior Choir Member at the New First Baptist Church Taylorsville in Portsmouth, Va. She passed away in August, 2009.

My oldest sister, Alveta Loray Jones, was born March 22, 1959 at the Portsmouth Naval Hospital. She graduated with honors from Manor High School in 1976. She received her Bachelor's degree in Accounting from Virginia Commonwealth University (VCU) in 1980. She married Roland K. Jones in 1983 and they have a daughter named Chavia. They currently reside in Atlanta. My youngest sister, Michelle, was born February 6, 1969 at the Portsmouth Naval Hospital. She graduated with honors from I.C. Norcom High School in 1987. She attended Hampton University. She married James Wiggins, Sr. in 1992 and they have a son named James Jr. and a daughter named Jazmine. They currently reside in Portsmouth.

My wife, Sonja F. Sharpe, was born March 28, 1967 in Brooklyn, NY. Her family moved to Greensboro, NC when she was eleven. She graduated from Dudley High School in 1985 and received her Bachelor's degree in Clinical Social Work from North Carolina A&T. She is currently pursuing her Master's degree in Clinical Social Work from Norfolk State University. My son, Brandon Queron Maloney, was born June 10, 1999 at Roosevelt Roads Military Hospital in Puerto Rico. He is currently living in Jacksonville, Florida with his mother. Brandon is a great, fun-loving kid who excels in sports and academics. His favorite sport is basketball.

Now let me give you a quick summary of my 22-year military career in the U.S. Army. I am a Distinguished Military Graduate (DMG) from North Carolina Agricultural and State University in Greensboro, where I earned a Bachelor's of

Science degree in Architectural Engineering in 1990. I was commissioned a second lieutenant in the U.S. Army Corps of Engineers. My first assignment was with the 12th Engineer Battalion, 1st Armored Division (Mechanized) in Mannheim, Germany. I served as a Platoon Leader, Company Executive Officer, and Battalion Training Officer. Following my tour in Germany, I attended the Engineer Officer Advance Course at Fort Leonard Wood, Missouri. After the Engineer Officer Advance Course, I was assigned to 20th Engineer Brigade (Combat) (Airborne) at Fort Bragg as the Brigade Assistant Operations Officer. I was later assigned to the 37th Engineer Battalion (Combat) (Airborne) where I served as the Battalion Adjutant and Charlie Company Commander. Following my first tour at Fort Bragg, I was assigned to 2d-348th CS Battalion at Fort Buchanan, Puerto Rico, where I was the Senior Engineer Observer Control / Trainer. I was then assigned to 3rd Army/ARCENT at Fort McPherson, Georgia as the C7 Construction Division Chief. In November 2001, I deployed to Kuwait and Afghanistan with the ARCENT Forward Headquarters in support of Operation Enduring Freedom. I returned to Fort Bragg, where I served as the Deputy of Joint Exercises, 18th Airborne Corps, followed by Brigade Operations Officer and Executive Officer of the 20th Engineer Brigade (Combat) (Airborne). While in those positions, I twice deployed to Iraq in support of Operation Iraqi Freedom. In June 2005, I was assigned to the 2d Battalion-362th Field Artillery Regiment at Fort Carson, Colorado, where I served as the Battalion Executive Officer. I was then assigned to Fort Monroe, Virginia, where I served as the Senior Joint Doctrine Developer. I was later selected to serve as the Division Engineer of the 2nd Infantry Division, Camp Red Cloud, South Korea. My final active duty assignment was at the Joint Forces Staff College in Norfolk, where I served as a Military Faculty/Instructor in the Joint and Combined Warfighting School. I am a graduate of the U.S. Army Corps of Engineer's Officer Basic and Advance Courses, the Army Command and General Staff College, the Command Arms and Services Staff School Course (CAS3), Scout Platoon Leaders Course, Jumpmaster Course, and Airborne School. My awards and decorations include the Meritorious Service Medal (four awards), the Army Commendation Medal, the Joint Service Achievement Medal, the Iraqi Campaign Medal, the Army Achievement Medal (two awards), the National Defense Service Medal (two medals), the Global War on Terrorism Medal, the Humanitarian Service Medal (two medals), and the Senior Parachutist Badge.

Part II
History of African-Americans in the U.S. Military

"For more than two hundred years, African-Americans have participated in every conflict in United States history. They have not only fought bravely the common enemies of the United States but have also had to confront the individual and institutional racism of their countrymen."

— Lt. Col. [Ret] Michael Lee Lanning, author, "The African-American Soldier: From Crispus Attucks to Colin Powell."

REVOLUTIONARY WAR

Crispus Attucks

March 5th, 1770 is a date that will never be forgotten. The story of Crispus Attucks is still taught in classes throughout America today. Attucks would go down as a martyr for the American Revolution. The event would inspire rebellion in people throughout the New World. Attucks was born around 1723 in Massachusetts to an African father and Indian mother. Not much else is really known about Crispus until the fateful day.

The day began like any other, until a commotion was heard in the streets and Attucks went to investigate. Upon arriving, he discovered a fight brewing between some Boston men and British soldiers. Attucks went to the front of the crowd and struck one of the British soldiers. He was immediately fired upon. Five colonists would be killed during the ensuing fire and six were wounded. The surviving colonists gathered the bodies and carried them away, to be held until a funeral could be arranged. A few days later, businesses closed so that all could attend the funerals of the killed men. Historians have debated whether

Attucks was a hero or a villain, but there is no doubt that he was the first person to die in the American Revolution. Attucks' actions stirred up patriotic fervor and compelled all colonists to rebel against the British.

Facts...

- About 5,000 Blacks fought against the British
- Those who fought for the British Army faced persecution and death as traitors
- Black soldiers after the war were still not recognized as qualified soldiers due to the racial divide
- Blacks were allowed to enlist because Army commanders feared that the Army was not large enough to defeat the British

---

1770: Crispus Attucks

On March 5, 1770, Crispus Attucks and several other patriots from Boston protested the British curbing of civil liberties in their Massachusetts colony.

During a scuffle with British soldiers, Attucks and several others were shot and killed. Although independence had not yet been officially declared, many consider Attucks the first American casualty of the Revolutionary War.

The Boston Massacre greatly helped to foster colonists' spirit of independence from Great Britain. More than 5,000 blacks—both slave and free—would later take up the cause and fight for America's independence. Unfortunately, freedom for most of them would have to wait.

1775

African-Americans participated on the patriot side in the earliest battles of the American Revolution, including those at Concord, Lexington and Bunker Hill. Two of these patriot soldiers were Peter Salem at the Battle of Concord and Salem Poor at the Battle of Bunker Hill. General George Washington reversed his earlier policy of rejecting the services of slaves and free blacks in the army. Five thousand African-Americans served during the Revolutionary War, including two predominantly black units in Massachusetts, one in Connecticut, one in Rhode Island.

THE CIVIL WAR

The 54th Massachusetts Infantry

One of the first black units to join the Union forces in the Civil War was the 54th, a unit with the eyes of the nation upon it. The company, which was largely composed of freed black slaves from various northern states, earned its fame in the Battle at Fort Wagner on July 18, 1863. It was assigned the challenge of leading the assault on this Confederate fort, which was located on an island near Charleston, S.C. Although the unsuccessful attack resulted in heavy casualties, the courageous act of one member of Company C brought the 54th widespread attention. During the battle, the unit managed to briefly capture a small section of the battery. However, the unit's leader, Col. Robert Gould Shaw, was fatally wounded in the process. Seeing that the color sergeant was down, Sgt. William H. Carney risked his life to take the flag and lead the troops to the parapet, upon which he planted the colors. When the soldiers were given the order to retreat, Carney again took the flag while facing heavy fire before falling back. He was severely wounded by two bullets during the battle but survived to become the first African-American to be presented a Congressional Medal of Honor, on May 23, 1900.[1]

Facts...

- In the beginning, the North and South both opposed Blacks enlisting
- Blacks were not allowed to enlist in the Union Army until 1862
- Over 100,000 black soldiers would enlist for the Union
- The South used Blacks for heavy labor deemed necessary to rage war on the Union
- Only 100 blacks were commissioned during the war
- In the end, six regular Army regiments of black troops were formed and led by white officers
- West Point and the Naval Academy were required to accept black cadets and midshipmen, but refused to commission black officers

- 1870-1898: 23 blacks were appointed to West Point. Only twelve attended. Six stayed longer than one semester, and only three graduated
- The first black graduate from West Point was Lieutenant Henry O. Flipper, class of 1877. The second was Lieutenant John Alexander (1887) and the third was Lieutenant Charles Young (1889—retired as a full colonel)
- Lieutenant Benjamin O. Davis became the Army's first black General in October of 1940 (he became a lieutenant in 1901 after passing an officers' qualification test)

INDIAN CAMPAIGNS

Buffalo Soldiers

After the Civil War, Congress authorized the creation of six segregated black regiments to serve in the peace-time army under white officers. The Ninth and Tenth Cavalries and the 38th through 41st Infantries—all composed of African-American soldiers—were thus formed.

The new cavalries were mainly stationed in the Southwest and the Great Plains, where it was their responsibility to build forts and maintain order in a frontier overrun by outlaws and occupied by Native Americans battling land-grabbing intruders. The black troops earned the nickname "Buffalo Soldiers" from Cheyenne Indians—as much for their ability in battle as for their dark skin. The men of the Ninth and Tenth Cavalries further proved their abilities in the Spanish-American War and in guarding the Mexican border. Members of both regiments fought in Cuba, participating in the battle at San Juan Hill. The Tenth also served under General John J. Pershing in the expedition against Mexican revolutionary Pancho Villa. In 1941, the two regiments merged to form the Fourth Cavalry Brigade, which was led by the Army's first African-American general, Benjamin O. Davis, Sr. The Fourth would exist for only three years before all horse cavalry regiments were disbanded.

WORLD WAR I

369th Regiment and the French Croix de Guerre

The 369th Regiment was reorganized and redesignated on March 1, 1918, and would not demobilize until February 28, 1919. The regiment would be involved in four different campaigns and suffer over 1,500 causalities during that time. This regiment was the first all Black regiment during WWI. The Regiment was initially assigned to the French Army for the duration of the war. During this time, the Regiment would capture the all-important village of Séchault, which would win them the French Croix de Guerre. The Regiment would continue to advance until they reached the banks of the Rhine River, becoming the first Allied unit to reach that objective.

Throughout the campaign, many of the members of the Regiment received Distinguished Service Crosses. One soldier, CPL Freddie Stowers, received a Medal of Honor. Another two that stand out from the Regiment, are the two men who received the Croix de Guerre, PVTs Henry Johnson and Needham Roberts.

Facts...

- Blacks supplied 13% of inductees during the Great War
- 350,000 blacks served in segregated units, mostly as support personnel
- Henry Johnson and Needham Roberts of the 369th became the first Americans of any race to receive the French Croix de Guerre
- Military commanders did much to discredit Blacks during this time, resulting in a decline in the number of Blacks within the military
- Blacks also began to demand the right to serve not only in combat, but under command of black officers
- On October 15th, 1917, about 639 men graduated from Fort Des Moines (which was designated as a training camp for blacks who wished to become officers) and were commissioned as captain or 1st and 2nd lieutenant
- Over 1300 blacks would be commissioned during the war
- Many white soldiers refused to salute black officers

WORLD WAR II

The Tuskegee Airmen

By the beginning of World War II, African-Americans were placing increased pressure on the government to make conditions more equal for blacks in the Armed Forces. While reluctant to fully integrate the military, the government took a step forward in 1941 by creating the first all-black military aviation program at the Tuskegee Institute in Alabama. The action received a great deal of criticism from black Americans who were outraged by their continued segregation. In May 1943, the first group of Tuskegee-trained pilots was sent to North Africa to join the Allied forces. They were headed by Capt. Benjamin O. Davis, Jr., who would later become the first African-American Air Force general. The accomplishments made by the 99th Fighter Squadron, especially in it's collaboration with the all-white 79th Fighter Group in October 1943, helped pave the way for integration in the Air Force.

The Tuskegee Airmen were the first group of black fighter pilots allowed into the US Army Air Corps in World War II. (US Army Signal Corps/Associated Press/File 1942)

KOREAN WAR

The End of Segregation

Blacks have faced a litany of discrimination within the civilian and military arenas. While the military struggled to find a balance between admitting black officers and empowering them to command white soldiers, many black officers were denied the rights given to white officers. White subordinates were not forced to salute black officers, and for that manner, black officers could not give commands to white soldiers. The military gradually realized that, as times progressed and blacks proved themselves again and again, the segregation which ran rampant through the ranks would no longer work. The end of segregation came toward the end of the Korean War with President Truman's Executive Order 9981. The tide seemed to change when, in June, 1947, President Truman stated in a speech on civil rights and human freedom that "it is my deep conviction that we have reached a turning point in the long history of our efforts to guarantee a freedom and equality to all our citizens...And when I say all Americans—I mean all Americans." Eight months later, President Truman would send Congress a message on Civil Rights that proposed a ten-point program that included a multitude of initiatives, one of which called for the desegregation of the Armed Forces. Congress easily blocked the President's proposal. However, the issue would rise once again in July of that year. Though Truman continued to face resistance in civil rights legislation, he decided to use an executive order to desegregate the Armed Forces. Executive Order 9981 declared a policy of equal opportunity regardless to race, religion, or national origin. The order also created a seven-member committee on the Equality of Treatment in the Armed Services and deemed that all government agencies at all levels would comply with the committee. Thus, by the end of the Korean War in 1953, the military was almost completely desegregated and the last all black unit was disbanded in 1954. Thus the Army's integration of black and white units at the end of the Korean War was the first department of the government and really the first element of society to have an integrated workforce. The Army and the armed services would become a model for the rest of the country to follow ten years later in finally giving African-Americans the same right.

Facts...

- One of the first ground units was the all black 24th Regiment
- Only 15% of the Army's force was black in Korea
- The war marked the beginning of military integration
- July 26th, 1951- General Matthew B. Ridgway received approval to integrate all troops
- By the end of the war, over 200,000 blacks had enlisted
- By the end of 1954, the last all-black unit had been disbanded and black enlistees were accepted without a quota system

---

VIETNAM WAR

The Call for Blacks

Just as changes had been seen in the Armed Forces at the end of the Korean War for blacks, the same was happening in America. In 1964, the Civil Rights Bill was passed, which banned discrimination of blacks in all sectors. By the end of that year, the U.S. had sent over 180,000 soldiers to fight the Viet Cong in Vietnam. The military deemed it necessary to step up recruiting and heavily targeted men and women, black and white. Many chose to serve as a way to gain respect from whites in showing that they too would defend the country. Though blacks only constituted 11% of the population, they would make up almost 13% of the fighting force in Vietnam. Just prior to the outbreak of war, President John F. Kennedy realized that though blacks made up a significant percentage of the population, they were not well-represented throughout the Armed Forces. The President called for research on how to change recruiting and direct it toward attracting more blacks into service. However, tensions began to rise in Vietnam and the issue was set aside. The draft did not discriminate between blacks and whites, and now blacks were being drafted by the thousands. Blacks were at a distinct disadvantage with the draft because men could defer if they were attending college or if they held certain civilian occupations. More white males were in college or held these positions. Blacks were also more likely to be slotted into combat positions and had a higher death rate than any other race fighting, accounting for over 15% of all combat-related deaths. Fifteen blacks would be awarded the Medal of Honor for their actions in the conflict. While many blacks fought in Vietnam, the rest were fighting back home for their civil rights. Once they were granted, they fought for acceptance of their rights by the rest of the country.

Facts...

- Blacks were among the first to receive Medals of Honor
- CPT Elizabeth Allan, a nurse in the Army Nurse Corps, volunteered to go to Vietnam
- Racial integration in the military was met with better success than in other institutions in the United States (Civil Rights Movement)
- 1962 – only 1.6% of officers were black

MILITARY INTEGRATION TIMELINE

The integration of the Armed Forces was a momentous event in our military and national history. It represented a milestone in the development of the Armed Forces and the fulfillment of the democratic ideal. The existence of integrated, rather than segregated, Armed Forces is an important factor in our military establishment. The experiences of World War II and the postwar pressures generated by the civil rights movement compelled all the services to reexamine their traditional practices of segregation. While there were differences in the ways that the services moved toward integration, all were subject to the same demands, fears, and prejudices and had the same need to use their resources in a more rational and economical way. All of them reached the same conclusion: traditional attitudes toward minorities must give way to democratic concepts of civil rights.

1945

The United States declares victory over Japan on Aug. 15, effectively ending World War II; a war in which more than 900,000 African-Americans served. In October, Army Lt. Gen. Alvan C. Gillem Jr. is appointed to study the Army's race policies and prepare a directive for post-war black soldiers. In November, the Gillem Board makes eighteen recommendations to improve the Army's employment and treatment of black soldiers.

1946

The Army and Navy adopt policies of integration and equal rights for black service members, though the policies were not widely implemented or enforced. War Secretary Robert P. Patterson directs military-wide acceptance of the new policies in April. But as services continue to challenge integration, Patterson suspends black enlistments in the regular Army in July. Meanwhile, racial turmoil across the United States prompts President Harry S. Truman in September to establish a civil rights committee to investigate racial violence – a decision that becomes the catalyst for widespread military integration over the next decade.

1947

Policies and practices within the services lead to a significant decline in black enlistment and retention. Meanwhile, there is progress in targeted areas. Lt. Gen. Clarence Huebner develops a program that trains thousands of black soldiers serving in Europe. The Army Air Force closes its last segregated officer training program at Tuskegee Airfield in favor of integrated classes. Civil rights leader A. Philip Randolph forms the Committee Against Jim Crow in the Military. In October, the President's Committee on Civil Rights recommends sweeping reforms that include using the military "as an instrument of social change" by ending segregation of the services.

1948

In February, Truman refers the recommendations of the civil rights committee to Congress. In April, Defense Secretary James V. Forrestal tells black leaders that while he agrees with their quick goals for integration, his gradual approach is best. In May, Lt. John E. Rudder becomes the first African-American to receive a regular commission in the Marine Corps. In June, Congress passes the Selective Service Act but refuses to act on segregation. Truman signs the bill and, following a racially-charged Democratic National Convention that nominated him for a second term as president, signs Executive Order 9981. The order is largely ignored by the services for months.

1949

In February, the Department of Defense's new Personnel Policy Board drafts policies to abolish all racial quotas, establish uniform draft standards, and fully integrate the services by July 1, 1950. The policies are not approved. In March, the Fahy Committee, which Truman appointed to implement integration, states that its goal is to convince service leaders of the merits of integration, rather than to impose it on them. In April, newly-appointed Defense Secretary Louis Johnson issues a policy affirming Truman's integration order. Under increasing pressure from Johnson, the Air Force issues a "bill of rights" for black airmen, and the Navy proposes a recruiting program to enlist black sailors. By September, post-war downsizing leads the Marine Corps to eliminate its segregated training platoons and various on-post facilities.

1950

In January, the Army drops its longstanding defense of discriminatory practices by publishing a list of job vacancies that, for the first time, were to be filled without regard to race. Still, the Air Force leads in implementing integration by changing from 106 black units and 167 integrated units to 89 black units and 350 integrated units within a month. Forced by the necessities of war, the 1st Provisional Marine Brigade is assigned several African-Americans during the fighting on the Pusan Perimeter, marking the first time that black servicemen are integrated in significant numbers in combat.

1951

Although support for segregation was still widespread in the Army, the service's nine training divisions are integrated by March and black recruitment and retention is as much as 60% over authorization. Fort Ord in Monterey, California is the Army's first integrated training division. Fort Dix, New Jersey and Fort Knox, Kentucky are the last. Unlike in World War II, blacks are serving in combat at equal rates as whites in the Marine Corps, where at least half of black Marines in combat served in integrated units, earning much respect and commendation for fighting in Korea. Although African-Americans have participated in every major U.S. war, the battle for integration and recognition of the accomplishments of black soldiers has been a slow process. Credit to blacks in the military has gradually been awarded, often where long overdue. We have pinpointed just a few historical black regiments that exemplify the struggles and the contributions by African-Americans in the Armed Forces before integration.

Seven Blacks Finally Gain Recognition

Blacks began winning Medals of Honor during the Civil War. However, between the Civil War and World War II, none of the 300 men awarded this honor were black. In 1993, Shaw University conducted a study of Medal of Honor recipients and focused on the racial disparity in the Army. The study resulted in the recommendation to consider ten black soldiers for the Medal of Honor. Seven were ultimately recommended to receive the award. In 1996, Congress passed legislation which allowed the president to award the Medals of Honor. On January 13th, 1997 President Bill Clinton presented six of the medals to families of the deceased men. One soldier, 1LT Vernon Baker was present to receive his medal. Read more about each man's bravery and action in the Medal of Honor section. One of the deceased recipients, SSG Edward Carter, was exhumed and moved to rest in Arlington National Cemetery.

Part III
History of Black Women in the Military

A merican women have participated in the defense of this nation during times of war and peace. Their contributions, however, have gone largely unrecognized and unrewarded. While women in the United States Armed Forces share a history of discrimination based on gender, black women have also faced racial discrimination. Initially barred from official military status, black women persistently pursued their right to serve.

Early Patriots

No documented records have been discovered of black women's military service in the American Revolution. They may well have served alongside black men. During the Civil War, the service of black women included nursing or domestic chores in medical settings, laundering uniforms, and cooking for the soldiers. As the Union Army marched through the South and large numbers of freed black men enlisted, their female family members often obtained employment with the unit. The Union Army paid black women to raise cotton on plantations for the northern government to sell. Five black nurses served under the direction of Catholic nuns aboard the Navy hospital ship *Red Rover*. Four of their names – Alice Kennedy, Sarah Kinno, Ellen Campbell and Betsy Young – have been recorded.

Black nurses are in the record books of both Union and Confederate hospitals. As many as 181 black nurses—both female and male—served in convalescent and US government hospitals in Maryland, Virginia, and North Carolina during the war. Susie King Taylor, Civil War nurse, cook, and laundress, was raised as a slave on an island off the coast of Georgia. In April of 1861, Major General Hunter assaulted Fort Pulaski and freed all the slaves in the area, including Mrs. King. When Union officers raised the First South Carolina Volunteers (an all-black unit), Mrs. King signed on as laundress and nurse. Able to read and write, she also set up a school for black children and soldiers. Following the war, Mrs. King established another school for freed slaves. When her husband, Sergeant Edward King of the First South Carolina Volunteers, died in 1866, she collected a widow's pension. In 1879, she married Russell Taylor. For the remainder of her life, she continued her advocacy for black Civil War troops. Immediately following the Civil War, William Cathey enlisted in the United States Regular Army in St. Louis, Missouri. William Cathey, intending to serve three years with the 38th US Infantry, was described by the recruiting officer as 5-foot-9 with black eyes, black hair, and a black complexion. The cursory examination by an Army physician missed the fact that William was actually Cathay Williams, a woman. "William Cathey" served from November 15, 1866, until her discharge with a surgeon's certificate of disability on October 14, 1868. Despite numerous and often lengthy hospital stays during her service, her sex was not revealed until June 1891, when Cathay Williams applied for an invalid pension and disclosed her true identity. She did not receive the pension, not because she was a woman, but because her disabilities were not service related. Cathay was probably the first black woman to serve in the US Regular Army.[2]

Spanish-American War

Many black women served as nurses during the Spanish-American War. The yellow fever and typhoid epidemics led Surgeon General George Sternberg and Dr. Anita Newcomb McGee, Acting Assistant Surgeon in charge of nurses, to seek out female "immunes"—women who had survived the disease. On July 13, 1898, Namahyoke Curtis (wife of Dr. Austin Curtis, Superintendent of the Freedman's Hospital in Washington, D.C.) was asked to recruit immune nurses. Mrs. Curtis hired 32 black women who were allegedly immune to yellow fever. Most of her recruits went to Santiago, Cuba in July and August, 1898 to serve in the worst of the epidemics. At least two of their number, T.R. Bradford and Minerva Trumbull, died from typhoid fever. Other black graduate nurses received direct contracts from the Surgeon General for service in the Spanish-American War. Tuskegee Institute records reveal that five nursing graduates served in Army camps. Black women nurses were also recruited from Freedmen's Hospital in Washington D.C., Provident Hospital in Chicago, Massachusetts General, Charity Hospital in New Orleans, and the Phyllis Wheatley Training School. As many as 80 black women may have served.

World War I

At the outset of World War I, many trained black nurses enrolled in the American Red Cross hoping to gain entry into the Army or Navy Nurse Corps. As the war escalated, public pressure increased to enlist black women. Finally, eighteen black Red Cross nurses were offered Army Nurse Corps assignments shortly after the Armistice. They were assigned to Camp Grant, Illinois, and Camp Sherman, Ohio, where they lived in segregated quarters and cared for German prisoners of war and black soldiers. The cessation of hostilities halted plans to assign black nurses to Camp Dodge, Camp Meade, Fort Riley, and Camp Taylor. By August 1919, all black nurses had been released from service as the nursing corps was reduced to peacetime levels. Following the war, demand for a permanent place for black women nurses in the military nursing corps continued. Black women served their country in other capacities. Four black women were among the 3,480 "Y" women volunteers who helped soldiers and sailors overseas. At the request of the Army, the YMCA provided recreation for the American Expeditionary Force by staffing canteens, nursing, sewing, baking, and providing amusement and educational activities for the soldiers.

World War II

In January 1941, the Army opened its nurse corps to blacks, establishing a ceiling of 56 nurses. On June 25, 1941, President Roosevelt's Executive Order 8802 created the Fair Employment Practices Commission, which led the way in eradicating racial discrimination in the defense program. In June 1943, Frances Payne Bolton, a congresswoman from Ohio, introduced an amendment to the Nurse Training Bill to bar racial bias. Soon 2,000 blacks were enrolled in the Cadet Nurse Corps.

The quota for black Army Nurses was eliminated in July, 1944. More than 500 black Army nurses served stateside and overseas during the war. The Navy dropped its color ban on January 25, 1945, and on March 9, Phyllis Daley became the first black commissioned Navy nurse.

Black women also enlisted in the WAAC (Women's Army Auxiliary Corps), which soon converted to the WAC (Women's Army Corps), the Navy WAVES (Women Accepted for Volunteer Emergency Service), and the Coast Guard SPARS.

Courtsey of: National Archives

From its beginning in 1942, black women were part of the WAAC. When the first WAACs arrived at Fort Des Moines, Iowa, there were 400 white women and 40 black women. Dubbed "ten-percenters," recruitment of black women was limited to 10% of the WAAC population—matching the black proportion of the national population. Enlisted women served in segregated units, participated in segregated training, lived in separate quarters, ate at separate tables in mess halls, and used segregated recreation facilities. Officers received their officer candidate training in integrated units, but lived under segregated conditions. Specialist and technical training schools were integrated in 1943. During the war, 6,520 black women served in the WAAC/WAC.

Courtsey of: U.S. Army

Black women were barred from the WAVES until October 19, 1944. The efforts of Director Mildred McAfee and Dr. Mary McLeod Bethune helped Secretary of the Navy James Forrestal push through their admittance. The first two black WAVES officers, Harriet Ida Pikens and Frances Wills, were sworn in December 22, 1944. Of the 80,000 WAVES in the war, a total of 72 black women served, normally under integrated conditions. The Coast Guard opened the SPARS (from the Coast Guard motto Semper Paratus, "Always Ready") to black members on October 20, 1944, but only a few actually enlisted.[3]

The Path to Full Integration

Following World War II, racial and gender discrimination and segregation persisted in the military. Entry quotas and segregation in the WAC deterred many from re-entry between 1946 and 1947. By June, 1948, only four black officers and 121 enlisted women remained in the WAC. President Truman eliminated the issues of segregation, quotas and discrimination in the armed forces by signing Executive Order 9981. WACs began integrated training and living in April, 1950. Meanwhile, on January 6, 1948, Ensign Edith De Voe was sworn into the Regular Navy Nurse Corps and in March, First Lieutenant Nancy C. Leftenant entered the Regular Army Nurse Corps, becoming the corps' first black members. Affirmative action and changing racial policies opened new doors for black women. During the Korean and Vietnam Wars, black women took their places in the war zone.

Courtsey of: U.S. Army

On July 15, 1964, Margaret E. Bailey became the first black nurse promoted to Lieutenant Colonel in the Army Nurse Corps. She would later become the first black Colonel. Hazel W. Johnson became the first black female general officer on September 1, 1979, when she assumed the position of Chief of the Army Nurse Corps.

1948 First Lieutenant Nancy C. Leftenant was the first black woman to become a member of the Regular Army Nurse Corps in March—she had joined the Reserve Corps in February, 1945.

1951 The first three black women commissioned as officers (Second Lieutenants) in the Air Force were Edwina Martin of Danville, Virginia; Fannie Jean Cotton of Jackson, Michigan; and Evelyn M. Brown of Shreveport, Louisiana. All three graduated from the Air Force Officer Candidate School at Lackland Air Force Base, Texas.

1964 Margaret E. Bailey, Army Nurse Corps, was the first nurse to be promoted to Lieutenant Colonel.

1967 Captain Clara Adams-Ender became the first female in the US Army to qualify for and be awarded the Expert Field Medical Badge.

1969 Captain Diane Lindsay, Army Nurse Corps, was the first black nurse to receive the Soldier's Medal for Heroism.

1970 Lieutenant Colonel Margaret E. Bailey, Army Nurse Corps, became the first black nurse to hold the rank of Colonel.

1972 Mildred C. Kelly became the first black female E9 (Sergeant Major) in the US Army.

1974 Staff Sergeant Joyce B. Malone became the first black woman to earn Airborne Wings in the US Army Reserves.

1976 Lieutenant Colonel Clara Adams-Ender became the first woman in the US Army to earn the Master of Military Art and Science degree from the Army Command and General Staff College at Fort Leavenworth, Kansas.

1979 Brigadier General Hazel W. Johnson-Brown became the first black female general officer and the first black Chief of the Army Nurse Corps.

1987 Irene Trowell-Harris became the first black female general officer in the National Guard.

1995 Brigadier General Marcelite Harris, USAF, was promoted to major general, the first black woman to attain this rank.

1997 US Army Sergeant Danyell Wilson became the first black woman to earn the prestigious job of guarding the Tomb of the Unknowns at Arlington National Cemetery.

Black Women in the Modern Military: Honoring Black Women's Service

Courtsey of: The Women's Memorial

Charity Adams Earley, commander of the 6888th Central Postal Directory Battalion in World War II, summarized the history of women in the military when she wrote in 1989:

> *The future of women in the military seems assured.... What may be lost in time is the story of how it happened. The barriers of sex and race were, and sometimes still are, very difficult to overcome, the second even more than the first. During World War II women in the service were often subject to ridicule and disrespect even as they performed satisfactorily.... Each year the number of people who shared the stress of these accomplishments lessens. In another generation young black women who join the military will have scant record of their predecessors who fought on the two fronts of discrimination—segregation and reluctant acceptance by males.*

Desert Storm

African-American women served with distinction during Operation Desert Storm as officers, noncommissioned officers, and enlisted soldiers. Of the 35,000 females who participated in Desert Storm, an estimated 40% were African-Americans. One African-American woman, LT Phoebe Jeter, who headed an all-male platoon, ordered numerous Patriots (anti-missile missiles) to be fired at several Iraqi surface-to-surface scud missiles. Another African-American woman, CPT Cynthia Mosely, commanded Alpha Company, 24th Support Battalion Forward, 24th Infantry Division (Mechanized), a 100-person unit that supplied everything from fuel to water to ammunition. Her unit resupplied fuel for all of the forward brigades because it was closest to the front lines. Brigadier General Hazel W. Johnson-Brown, USA NG (Ret.), a groundbreaker herself, told attendees at the Groundbreaking Ceremony for the Women in Military Service for America Memorial on June 22, 1995,

> *In the past, women, particularly minority women, have always responded when there was a crisis or need. We acknowledge all minority women in uniform, both present in this audience and not present. You are the strength of our success. You represent the patchwork quilt of diversity which is America—race, creed, color and ethnicity.*

Military Firsts

- March 8, 1945, **Phyllis Mae Daily**, the first Black nurse, was sworn into the Navy Nurse Corps in New York City.
- February 12, 1948, the first Black nurse joined the Regular Army Nurse Corps.
- In July 1974, **Reverend Alice Henderson** was commissioned as a chaplain, becoming the first female chaplain of any race.
- Also in July 1974, five Black women out of a group of fifteen became cadets at the U.S. Merchant Marine Academy.
- In May 1975, **Lieutenant Donna P. Davis** became the first Black female doctor in the Naval Medical Corps.[4]
- In November 1979, **Second Lieutenant Marcella A. Hayes** became the 55th woman out of 48,000 officers to graduate from the Army Aviation School in Ft. Rucker, Alabama. She became the first Black woman pilot in the U.S. Armed Forces.

- In September 1979, **Hazel Winifred Johnson** became the first Black woman promoted to the rank and position of Brigadier General, Chief of the Army Nurse Corps.
- In December 1980, **Ensign Brenda Robinson** became the first Black female aviator in the U.S. Navy assigned to the Fleet Logistics Squadron Forty in Norfolk, Virginia.
- On May 18, 1983, **Angela Dennis** of Arkansas became one of the first two Black women to graduate from the United States Coast Guard Academy in New London, Connecticut.

Part IV
Notable African-American Officers in the U.S. Army

T his Chapter is full of African-Americans who met challenges head-on. They showed that African-Americans possess the ability to serve in the capacity of General Officer. These are individuals who seized a time to make a difference and helped lead African-Americans in the Armed Forces to a much higher profile in history.

BENJAMIN OLIVER DAVIS, SR.

The First African-American General Officer in the Regular Army and in the U.S. Armed Forces

Biography

Benjamin O. Davis, Sr., was born in Washington, D.C. on July 1, 1877. He entered military service on July 13, 1898 during the War with Spain as a temporary first lieutenant of the 8th United States Volunteer Infantry. He was mustered out on March 6, 1899, and on June 18, 1899, he enlisted as a private in Troop I, 9th Cavalry, of the Regular Army. He then served as corporal and squadron sergeant major and, on February 2, 1901, was commissioned as 2nd lieutenant of Cavalry in the Regular Army.

Promotions

He was promoted to 1st lieutenant on March 30, 1905, to captain on December 24, 1915, to major (temporary) on August 5, 1917, and to lieutenant colonel (temporarily) on May 1, 1918. He reverted to his permanent rank of captain on October 14, 1919, and was promoted to lieutenant colonel on July 1, 1920, to colonel on February 18, 1930, and to brigadier general (temporarily) on October 25, 1940. He was retired on July 31, 1941, and recalled to active duty with the rank of brigadier general the following day.

Service

His first service as a commissioned officer of the Regular Army was in the Philippine Islands with the 9th Cavalry on the Island of Samar. In August 1901, he was assigned to duty with the 2nd Squadron, 10th Cavalry, and returned from the Philippines with that organization for service as Adjutant at Fort Washakie, Wyoming. In September 1905, he was made Professor of Military Science and Tactics at Wilberforce University, Ohio, where he remained until September 1909. After a brief tour of duty at Fort Ethan Allen, Vermont, he was detailed as Military Attaché to Monrovia, Liberia, until January, 1912. He was then assigned to duty with the 9th Cavalry at Fort D.A. Russell (predecessor of Fort Francis E. Warren), Wyoming and at Douglas, Arizona. He remained with his regiment on border patrol duty until February 1915, when he again was assigned to duty as Professor of Military Science and Tactics at Wilberforce. He remained there until the summer of 1917, when he went to the Philippines for duty as Supply Officer of the 9th Cavalry at Camp Stotsenburg. He returned to the United States in July 1920, and was assigned to duty as Professor of Military Science and Tactics at Tuskegee Institute. He served there until July 1924, when he became

Instructor of the 372nd Infantry, Ohio National Guard, stationed at Cleveland, Ohio. In July 1929, he returned to Wilberforce University as Professor Military Science and Tactics, serving until late 1930 when he was detailed on special duty with the Department of State in connection with affairs relating to the Republic of Liberia. In late 1931, he was assigned again to serve as Professor of Military Science and Tactics at Tuskegee, Alabama, where he remained until August 1937, when he was transferred to Wilberforce University. During the summers of 1930 to 1933, he was placed on detached service for duty with the Pilgrimage of War Mothers and Widows, making frequent trips to Europe on behalf of that organization. For his work on this assignment, he received letters of commendation from the Secretary of War and from the Quartermaster General. In August 1937 he was transferred from Tuskegee Institute to Wilberforce University. A year later, he was assigned as instructor and Commanding Officer of the 369th Infantry, New York National Guard. This organization was later changed to the 369th Coast Artillery (Anti-aircraft) Regiment. In January 1941 he was ordered to Fort Riley, Kansas for duty as a brigade commander with the 2nd Cavalry Division. The following June he was assigned to Washington, D.C. for duty as Assistant to the Inspector General. He was assigned to the European Theater of Operations in September 1942 on special duty as Advisor on Negro problems, and upon completion of this special duty, he returned to the United States and resumed his duties in the Inspector General's Department. In November 1944 he became Special Assistant to the Commanding General, Communications Zone, European Theater of Operations, stationed in Paris, France. A year later he was granted a period of detached service for the purposes of recuperation and rehabilitation. In January 1946 he again became Assistant to the Inspector General, serving once again in Washington, D.C. He retired on July 14, 1948, after having served his country for fifty years. General Davis died on November 26, 1970. His remains are interred in Arlington National Cemetery, Arlington, Virginia. His son, Lieutenant General Benjamin O. Davis, Jr., (U.S. Air Force, Retired), is the fourth African-American graduate of the U.S. Military Academy and the nation's second African American general officer.

Decorations and Honors

General Davis' U.S. military decorations consist of the Bronze Star Medal and the Distinguished Service Medal (DSM). His DSM medal, awarded by General Order 10, dated February 22, 1945, stated that General Benjamin O. Davis was awarded the DSM "for exceptionally meritorious service to the Government in a duty of great responsibility from June 1941 to November 1944. The War Department release issued about General Davis' DSM on February 11, 1945 included the following citation:

> *For exceptionally meritorious service to the Government in a duty of great responsibility from June, 1941, to November, 1944, as an Inspector of troop units in the field, and as special War Department consultant on matters pertaining to Negro troops. The initiative, intelligence and sympathetic understanding displayed by him in conducting countless investigations concerning individual soldiers, troop units and other components of the War Department brought about a fair and equitable solution to many important problems which have since become the basis of far-reaching War Department policy. His wise advice and counsel have made a direct contribution to the maintenance of soldier morale and troop discipline and has been of material assistance to the War Department and to responsible commanders in the field of understanding personnel matters as they pertain to the individual soldier.*

Additionally, General Davis was awarded an Honorary Degree of LL.D. from Atlanta University. His foreign awards and honors consisted of the Croix de Guerre with Palm from France and the Grade of Commander of the Order of the Star of Africa from Liberia.[5]

MAJ. GEN MARCIA M. ANDERSON

First Black Female Major General

Major General Marcia M. Anderson has commanded at the Company level through General Officer. She has also served in a variety of staff positions at Battalion, Brigade, and Division level, including S-1, S-3, S-4, and G-1, as well as an Assistant Division G-3. In July 2005, she assumed Command of the 6th Brigade, 95th Division (Institutional Training), where she was responsible for the 95th Division (Institutional Training) Drill Sergeant School located at Fort Sill, Oklahoma, as well as the conduct of Intermediate Level Education (ILE) and Combined Arms Exercise courses for officer professional development over an eight-state area. In June 2006, General Anderson was appointed acting Assistant Division Commander-Operations for the 95th Division (Institutional Training) in Oklahoma City. In April 2007 she was confirmed for promotion to Brigadier General, and in October 2007, she assumed command of the 85th Support Command (Regional Support Group West), Arlington Heights, Illinois. This command supports the collective training efforts of First Army. General Anderson was later named Deputy Commanding General-Support of First Army West. She assumed responsibility as Deputy Commander of the U.S. Army Human Resources Command on October 1, 2010. Effective one year later, Major General Anderson was assigned as the Deputy Chief, Army Reserve (IMA) with duty at the Pentagon. Individual Mobilization Augmentee (IMA) positions perform special missions and projects and may also be ordered to active duty.

Her military education includes the Adjutant General Basic and Advance courses, Basic and Intermediate Government Auditing, Command and General Staff College Course, Advanced Joint Professional Military Education, Capstone, and the United States Army War College, where she was awarded a Master's Degree in Strategic Studies. General Anderson has a Bachelor of Arts in Political Science from Creighton University and a juris Doctorate degree from Rutgers University School of Law. Her military awards and decorations include the Legion of Merit, Meritorious Service Medal (with three Oak Leaf Clusters), an Army Commendation Medal, an Army Achievement Medal, a Parachutist Badge, and a Physical Fitness Badge. As a citizen-soldier, General Anderson is employed by the United States Courts, where she serves as the Clerk of Bankruptcy Court, Western District of Wisconsin, located in Madison, Wisconsin. She is married to Amos Anderson.

LT. GEN. VINCENT K. BROOKS

Former Commanding General, Third Army/U.S. Army Central

On June 3rd, 2011 Lt. General Brooks took command of Third Army and Army Forces Central. The command is based at Shaw Air Force Base near Sumter, South Carolina, with portions of the command continuously deployed to the Middle Eastern countries of Kuwait, Qatar, Afghanistan, and Iraq. Brooks graduated from the United States Military Academy at West Point in 1980. He became the first black cadet in the school's history to be named cadet brigade commander (the top-ranking cadet). In this position, which is somewhat like the president of a college class, he led more than 4,000 cadets during his senior year. Brooks eventually graduated first in his class. During his 31 years as a commissioned officer, he served in command and staff positions in the United States, including in Germany during the Cold War, in Korea, Kosovo, and in the Middle East. His tours of duty with fighting units include the 82nd Airborne Division as a lieutenant; the 1st Infantry Division (Forward) as a captain; the 1st Cavalry Division as a major and again as a brigadier general; the 2nd Infantry Division as a lieutenant colonel; the Third Army Central (with duty in Headquarters, Coalition Joint Task Force - Kuwait) and the 3rd Infantry Division (with duty in North Atlantic Treaty Organization-Kosovo Forces) as a colonel; Headquarters, United States Central Command; Headquarters, 1st Cavalry Division (with duty as Headquarters, Multi-National Division-Baghdad) and Headquarters, III Corps and Fort Hood as a brigadier general; and the 1st Infantry Division (with duty as Headquarters U.S. Division - South) as a major general. General Brooks served at the national level in the Pentagon. Within Headquarters, Department of the Army, he fulfilled staff duties as aide-de-camp to the Vice Chief of Staff of the Army, and later as the Army's Chief of Public Affairs. Within the Joint Staff, he fulfilled duties as Deputy Director (J5) for Political-Military Affairs for the Western Hemisphere, and later as the Deputy Director (J5) for the War on Terrorism. General Brooks holds a Bachelor of Science degree from the United States Military Academy, a Master of Military Art and Science from the School of Advanced Military Studies at the United States Army Command and General Staff College, and an Honorary Doctor of Laws degree from the New England School of Law in Boston. He also served as a National Security Fellow at the Harvard University John F. Kennedy School of Government.

GEN. LLOYD J. AUSTIN III

Former Vice Chief of Staff of the U.S. Army

General Lloyd J. Austin III hails from Thomasville, Georgia. He was commissioned an Infantry 2nd lieutenant in 1975 upon graduation from the United States Military Academy. General Austin has served in a wide variety of command and staff positions throughout his 36-year career. His early assignments included duty with: the 1st Battalion, 7th Infantry, 3rd Infantry Division, U.S. Army Europe and Seventh Army; 2nd Battalion, 508th Infantry, 82nd Airborne Division at Fort Bragg, the U.S. Army Recruiting Battalion in Indianapolis, the United

States Military Academy,, the 2nd Battalion, 22nd Infantry and 1st Brigade, and the 10th Mountain Division (Light) at Fort Drum, New York. General Austin returned to Fort Bragg in 1993 and served as Commander, 2nd Battalion, 505th Parachute Infantry Regiment, 82nd Airborne Division, G-3 82nd Airborne Division, and later as the Commander, 3rd Brigade, 82nd Airborne Division from 1997 to 1999. Following duty at Fort Bragg, he was assigned to the Pentagon, where he served as Chief, Joint Operations Division, J-3 on the Joint Staff. More recently, General Austin served as the Assistant Division Commander (Maneuver), 3rd Infantry Division (Mechanized), Fort Stewart, Georgia and in Operation Iraqi Freedom from July 2001 until June 2003. He served as Commanding General, 10th Mountain Division (Light), Fort Drum, New York from September 2003 until August 2005 with duty as Commander, Combined Joint Task Force-180, Operation Enduring Freedom, Afghanistan. He then served as the Chief of Staff, United States Central Command, from September 2005 until November 2006, followed by assignment as the Commanding General, XVIII Airborne Corps in December 2006 where he commanded, Multi-National Corps—Iraq, Operation Iraqi Freedom, from February 2008 until April 2009. He was then assigned to the Pentagon as the Director, Joint Staff from August 2009 to August 2010. General Austin commanded United States Forces—Iraq from September 2010 through the completion of Operation New Dawn in December 2011.

His military education includes the Infantry Officer Advanced Course, United States Army Infantry School, Fort Benning, Georgia; United States Army Command and General Staff College, Fort Leavenworth, Kansas; and United States Army War College, Carlisle Barracks, Pennsylvania. He holds a Bachelor of Science degree from the United States Military Academy, a Master's degree in Education from Auburn University, and a Master's degree in Business Management from Webster University. General Austin's awards and decorations include the Defense Distinguished Service Medal (with three Oak Leaf Clusters), the Distinguished Service Medal (with Oak Leaf Cluster), the Silver Star, the Defense Superior Service Medal (with Oak Leaf Cluster), the Legion of Merit (with Oak Leaf Cluster), the Defense Meritorious Service Medal, the Meritorious Service Medal (with four Oak Leaf Clusters), the Joint Service Commendation Medal, the Army Commendation Medal (with six Oak Leaf Clusters), Army Achievement Medal (with Oak Leaf Cluster), Combat Action Badge, Expert Infantryman Badge, Master Parachutist Badge, the Ranger Tab and the Joint Chiefs of Staff Identification Badge.

MAJOR GENERAL BYRON S. BAGBY

**Former Operations Director,
Allied Joint Force Command Headquarters Brunssum**

Major General Bagby was commissioned through the Army ROTC Program at Westminster College in 1978. During his 31-year career, he has served as chief of the Middle East Division on the Joint Staff in the Directorate of Strategic Plans and Policy, J-5, assistant deputy director for politico-military affairs, and executive officer to the deputy chief of staff, G-8. Before assuming his current post in December 2009, he served as chief of staff and deputy commanding general of U.S. Army, NATO. From October 2006 until July 2008, he served as commandant of the Joint Forces Staff College, the Norfolk, Virginia wing of the National Defense University—America's premier joint military education institution. The college has educated officers from all military services in the art and profession of war fighting. Its mission is to instill in national security leaders a commitment to joint, multinational, and inter-agency teamwork, attitudes, and perspectives. Maj. Gen. Bagby has a master's degree from the University of North Carolina at Chapel Hill.

LIEUTENANT GENERAL JOE NATHAN BALLARD

Former Commandant and Chief of Engineers

Lieutenant General Joe Nathan Ballard is a former U.S. Army officer who fought in the Vietnam War, and who served for a time as Chief of Engineers. A native of Oakdale, Louisiana, Ballard was born on March 27, 1942. He graduated in 1965 from Southern University and A&M College in Baton Rouge with a degree in electrical engineering, after which he received a commission in the Corps of Engineers. Ballard served as a platoon leader in the 84th Engineer Battalion during his first tour of duty in Vietnam. He then returned to the United States and commanded a training company at Fort Polk. Later, he attended the Engineer Officer Advanced Course at Fort Belvoir before returning for his second tour in Vietnam as a company commander in the 864th Engineer Battalion and as the Chief, Lines of Communication Section in the 18th Engineer Brigade (Airborne). Following assignments with the Fifth U.S. Army and the Recruiting Command, he was Operations Officer and Executive Officer of the 326th Engineer Battalion, 101st Airborne Division. In 1978 he traveled to South Korea where he served as Operations Officer and later as the Executive Officer on the staff of the U.S. Forces in Korea. He returned to the Pentagon for duty on the Army Staff as the principal engineer in the Army Energy Office, Office of the Deputy Chief of Staff, Logistics. In 1982 he moved to another overseas theater as Commander of the 82nd Engineer Battalion, 7th Engineer Brigade, in West Germany. Later he became the Commander of the 18th Engineer Brigade and Assistant Deputy Chief of Staff, Engineer, in Headquarters, U.S. Army, Europe. Returning to the United States in 1991, Ballard became the Assistant Commandant of the U.S. Army Engineer School as Assistant Commandant of the Engineer School and Deputy Commanding General of the Engineer Center and Fort Leonard Wood, Missouri. After an assignment as Chief, Total Army Basing Study in the Office of the Chief of Staff of the Army, he returned to Missouri as Commanding General of the Engineer Center and Fort Leonard Wood. When Ballard was nominated by President Bill Clinton to be the Chief of Engineers and Commander, United States Army Corps of Engineers, he was serving as Chief of Staff, U.S. Army Training and Doctrine Command in Fort Monroe, Virginia. Ballard served as Chief of Engineers from October 1, 1996 until his retirement on August 2, 2000. During his career, Lieutenant General Ballard earned a Master's degree in Engineering Management from the University of Missouri – Rolla. He also graduated from the Engineer Officer Basic and Advanced Courses, the Command and General Staff College, and the Army War College.

BRIGADIER GENERAL BARBARANETTE T. BOLDEN

Former J-8, Mobility Assistant, Director of the Resources and Assessment Directorate, U. S. Pacific Command

Brigadier General Bolden earned her Bachelor's and Master's degrees in history from Arkansas State University. She enlisted as a member of the 567th Engineer Battalion of the Arkansas Army National Guard in 1975. Three years later, she headed to Washington, D.C. to study law at Howard University. While there she earned a commission through the District Guard Officer Candidate School. She has been climbing the Guard's management ladder ever since. Bolden was appointed chief of staff of the District of Columbia Army National Guard in 1999—the first female to be so appointed in the organization's history. Cognizant of the breakthrough for military women, she announced plans for a professional development mentoring program at the Army Guard Senior Leadership conference that same year. Brig. Gen. Bolden has served in numerous positions, including the following: director of personnel, commander, Land Component Command, and commander, Joint Task Force for the District of Columbia. Currently, she is responsible for assisting with planning and programming efforts to accomplish the U. S. Pacific Command's mission. She oversees experimentation, studies and analyses to fill the command's capability gaps.

LIEUTENANT GENERAL THOMAS P. BOSTICK

Former Deputy Chief of Staff G-1, U. S. Army

Lieutenant General Bostick graduated from the U.S. Military Academy in 1978 with a Bachelor of Science degree. He also holds a Master's degree in Civil Engineering and Mechanical Engineering. He has served in a variety of command and staff assignments in the U.S. and overseas, and was commanding general of the Gulf Region of the U.S. Army Corps of Engineers. He also served as assistant professor, Department of Mechanics at the U.S. Military Academy. More recently, he took control of the reserve and active-duty recruiting command and managed more than 8,000 military recruiters targeting young adults nationwide who wish to serve their country and see the military as an attractive option. Lt. Gen. Bostick was appointed top personnel leader on February 2, 2010. As G-1, he is the army's senior human resources decision maker. He develops, manages and executes all manpower/personnel plans, programs and policies across all components. The Army G-1 is responsible for training, coaching and mentoring, and fulfills the essence of the human resources mission. The Human Resources Command serves as the human resources provider and the key management, policy formulation, and process leader for the entire army.

BRIGADIER GENERAL ARNOLD N. GORDON-BRAY

Former Deputy Director, Operations,
U.S. Africa Command, Germany

Brigadier General Gordon-Bray, a 1978 alumnus of the University of Central Missouri and former member of the UCM basketball team, was the keynote speaker for the annual Freedom Scholarship Dinner January 19, 2010. The dinner raises funds for Martin Luther King Jr. Freedom Scholarships, presented annually to high school students from Johnson County, Missouri and the metropolitan Kansas City area, along with students currently enrolled at UCM. Brig.

Gen. Gordon-Bray was commissioned into the Infantry after graduation from UCM, and he was recognized as a Distinguished Military Student in UCM's ROTC program. He received a bachelor's degree from UCM and master's degrees in international strategic studies from the Air War College and the Naval War College. Prior to his current assignment, he completed his second tour in Iraq as the principal adviser to the Iraqi Ground Force Commander from 2006 to 2007.

BRIGADIER GENERAL ALBERT BRYANT, JR.

Former Director of Integration, Headquarters, Department of the Army, G8

Brigadier General Bryant was commissioned from the Military Academy in 1974. He attended graduate school at Stanford University, where, among others, the former Secretary of State Condoleezza Rice instructed him. Bryant was chief of the western hemisphere operations in the aftermath of the 9/11 attacks, and the assistant division commander of the 4th Infantry Division at the time of Sadaam Hussein's detection and capture.

BRIGADIER GENERAL JESSE R. CROSS

Former Quartermaster General and Commanding General, U.S. Army Quartermaster Center and School

Brigadier General Cross holds a Bachelor of Business Administration in marketing from West Texas State University and a Master of Science degree in logistics management from the Florida Institute of Technology. He was commissioned a 2nd lieutenant, Quartermaster Corps, through ROTC in 1979. He is a graduate of the Quartermaster Basic and Advanced Courses, the Command and General Staff College, and the U.S. Army War College. Brig. Gen. Cross was promoted to his current position in December 2005. H is the 50th Quartermaster general, with responsibility for training, doctrine and professional development of Quartermaster soldiers. The Quartermaster general also serves as the commanding general, Army Quartermaster Center and School, Fort Lee, Virginia and the traditional Quartermaster Regiment.

2ND LT. HENRY OSSIAN FLIPPER

First Black to Graduate from the U.S. Military Academy

Henry Ossian Flipper (March 12, 1856 – May 3, 1940) was an American soldier, former slave, and the first African-American to graduate from the United States Military Academy at West Point in 1877, earning a commission as a 2nd Lieutenant in the U.S. Army. Following Flipper's commission, he was transferred to one of the all-black regiments, serving in the U.S. Army which was historically led by white officers. Assigned to A Troop under the command of Captain Nicholas M. Nolan, he became the first non-white officer to lead Buffalo Soldiers of the 10th Cavalry. Flipper served with competence and distinction during the Apache Wars and the Victorio Campaign, but was haunted by rumors alleging improprieties. At one point he was court martialed and dismissed from the U.S. Army. After losing his commission in the Army, Flipper worked throughout Mexico and Latin America and as an assistant to the Secretary of the Interior. He retired to Atlanta in 1931 and died of natural causes in 1940. In 1976 his descendants applied to the U.S. military for a review of Flipper's court martial and dismissal. A review found that the conviction and punishment were "unduly harsh and unjust" and recommended that Flipper's dismissal be changed to a good conduct discharge. Shortly afterwards, an application for pardon was filed with the Secretary of the Army, which was forwarded to the Department of Justice. President Bill Clinton pardoned Lieutenant Henry O. Flipper on February 19, 1999.

MAJOR GENERAL (RET'D) GASKILL

General Gaskill was born in Yonkers, N.Y. on April 12, 1931, to John and Armania Gaskill. The Gaskill family later moved to Arlington, Va. General Gaskill completed Reserve Officer Training as a Distinguished Military Graduate, and received a bachelor of science in business administration from Howard University in 1952. He was commissioned into one of the last all-black battalions in the United States Army. General Gaskill had a distinguished and decorated career in the Army before his retirement in 1981, to which he credits the support of his late wife, Erotida Gaskill. General Gaskill is a Life Member of the NAACP, member of Unity in the Community, and an elder at his church.

MAJOR GENERAL MICHAEL T. HARRISON

Former Deputy Director for Requirements, J8, The Joint Staff

Major General Harrison entered the Army in May, 1980. Since then, he has served in a variety of Joint Staff and army staff positions, including assignment as a staff officer in the Counter-Narcotics Division, J-3, the Joint Staff. He assumed his current rank in August 2009. His most recent operational assignment was as deputy commanding general for the 10th Mountain Division (Light Infantry) at Fort Drum, New York. Previous assignments include service as a commander and staff officer with Air Assault, Light Infantry, and Training units, to include duties as deputy commanding general for the Combined Security Transition Command-Afghanistan. Maj. Gen. Harrison is a graduate of Howard University, where he earned a Bachelor of Arts Degree in English. He holds a Master of Science degree in General Administration from Central Michigan University, and a Master of Science in Strategic Studies from the U.S. Army War College, Carlisle Barracks, Pennsylvania.

BRIGADIER GENERAL SANFORD E. HOLMAN

Former Vice Commander, Joint Warfighting Center, Deputy Joint Force Trainer J-7

Army Reserve Brig. Gen. Holman has been nominated for appointment to the rank of major general. As a warrior-citizen, he has fourteen years of experience as a program and project manager, analyst, engineer, programmer, tester, and trainer for systems and software supporting the U.S. Army, Air Force and the intelligence community. He became vice commander of the Joint Warfighting Center and deputy joint force trainer at U.S. Joint Forces Command in 2008. While at JFCOM, he also served as the deputy commander for Combined Joint Task Force-950 for the U.S. Second Fleet. Brig. Gen. Holman graduated from the Military Academy and was commissioned in 1978. He returned to active duty in 2007 and deployed to Djibouti as the deputy commander—Horn of Africa. He remained on active duty following his return and was assigned to JFCOM. He is also serving on the secretary of the army's Reserve Forces Policy Committee. Brig. Gen. Holman is a graduate of the Army Command and General Staff College and the National War College. He holds two Master's degrees from the Florida Institute of Technology and the National Defense University.

LIEUTENANT GENERAL (RET'D) RUSSELL L. HONORÉ

Former Commanding General, U.S. First Army

Lieutenant General (Ret'd) Russell L. Honoré served as the 33rd commanding general of the U.S. First Army at Fort Gillem, Georgia. He is best known for serving as commander of Joint Task Force Katrina, responsible for coordinating military relief efforts for Hurricane Katrina-affected areas across the Gulf Coast, and as the 2nd Infantry Division Commander while stationed in Korea. He served until his retirement from the Army on January 11, 2008. Honoré is sometimes known as "the Ragin' Cajun", although he is actually of Louisiana Creole descent. The Honoré family surname is still found among the Cane River Créoles and in Pointe Coupee Parish. A native of Lakeland in Pointe Coupee Parish, Louisiana, and youngest of twelve children, Honoré earned a Bachelor of Science degree in Vocational Agriculture from Southern University and A&M College in 1971. He also holds a Master of Arts in Human Resources from Troy State University and an Honorary Doctorate in Public Administration from Southern University and A&M College. Honoré served in a variety of command and staff positions in Korea and Germany. He served as Commanding General, 2nd Infantry Division in South Korea; Vice Director for Operations, J-3, The Joint Staff, Washington, D.C.; Deputy Commanding General and Assistant Commandant, United States Army Infantry Center and School, Fort Benning, Georgia; and Assistant Division Commander, Maneuver/Support, 1st Cavalry Division, Fort Hood, Texas. Most recently, Honoré served as Commander, First United States Army.

BRIGADIER GENERAL CHARLES W. HOOPER

Former Deputy Director of Strategic Planning and Policy J-5, U.S. Pacific Command

Brigadier General Hooper is fluent in Mandarin, and has served several tours in China. Following his promotion to brigadier general, he was appointed U.S. defense attaché to the People's Republic of China, where he served from 2007 to 2009. Recently, the West Point graduate was the keynote speaker for an Achievement Week Banquet hosted by the Lambda Beta Beta chapter of Omega Psi Phi in Hawaii. Brig. Gen. Hopper served in Hawaii with the 25th Infantry Division from 1981 to 1983.

MAJOR GENERAL (RET'D) NATHANIEL JAMES

Former Commanding General of the
New York Army National Guard

Major General (Ret'd) Nathaniel James is the former commanding General of the New York Army National Guard. Born on July 25, 1935 in Branchville, South Carolina, his family migrated north to New York City during his childhood. James received early schooling in the New York City Public School system and attended Theodore Roosevelt High School before graduating from Bronx Vocational High School. James then enrolled at the State University of New York, earning his A.A. degree in Business and his B.A. degree in Political Science. After completing ROTC training in college and two years of enlisted service, James was commissioned as a 2nd lieutenant in 1959 through the Army Artillery and Missile School. During his 33-year career, James held a variety of positions and continued to develop his institutional knowledge of Army command, operations and strategy. James's military education includes the Army Artillery and Missile School; Army Transportation School; Army Command and General Staff College; Army War College; and the National Interagency Counter Drugs Institute. In 1975 James became the commander for the 369th Transportation Battalion, 42nd Division Artillery, and 42nd Division Support Command. Between 1988 and 1992, he served as the assistant adjutant general, Headquarters State Area Command, New York Army National Guard. Upon being promoted to Major General on December 29, 1992, James became the first African-American to obtain that rank in the history of the New York Army National Guard. In addition to previously commanding the 369th Transportation Battalion, James is the founder and president of both the 369th Veteran's Association, Inc. and the 369th Historical Society, Inc. The 369th Regiment was originally called the 15th New York Infantry and they were the first African-American regiment to engage in combat during World War II. After the war, 171 soldiers in that regiment were awarded the Croix de Guerre by the French Government, and German soldiers gave them the name "Harlem Hell Fighters" for the courage and valor they displayed in battle. James maintains hundreds of photographs and dozens of artifacts, papers, and other items to honor the legacy of the 369th Regiment. James's military decorations and awards include the Meritorious Service Medal, an Army Commendation, an Armed Forces Reserve Medal, the Army

Achievement Medal, the National Defense Medal, and the New York Humanitarian Service Medal.

BRIGADIER GENERAL LEODIS T. JENNINGS

Former Special Assistant to the Deputy Chief of Staff G8, Headquarters, Department of the Army

Brigadier General Jennings enlisted in 1975 and served as an armor crewman, gunner and tank commander. He earned his commission after completing the ROTC program at North Carolina State and graduating with a Bachelor of Science degree in Materials Engineering in 1983. His most recent assignment was as the operational assistant to the director, Army National Guard. He has served in various other senior level positions in the Army National Guard, including the G-3, and Chief, Force Management Division. Prior to his return to the Army National Guard Readiness Center in 2006, he served as Chief, Force Assessment in the Force Structure, Resources, and Assessment Directorate of the Joint Chiefs of Staff, where he developed analysis to assist in implementing the National Security Strategy. Brig. Gen. Jennings is a force manager and strategic planner, having served in numerous and varied positions at the Army National Guard Readiness Center, Headquarters, Department of the Army and the Joint Chiefs of Staff.

BRIGADIER GENERAL FREDERICK J. JOHNSON

Former Alabama Army National Guard

Brigadier General Johnson was commissioned 2nd lieutenant in the Army Reserve on December 16th, 1976 from ROTC at South Carolina State University. He entered active duty January 1977 at Ft. Knox, and was assigned to the Armor Officer Basic Course. He served in various active duty assignments from 1977 to 1988. Two years later, Brig. Gen. Johnson entered the Alabama Army National Guard, where he served in numerous staff positions in operations, training, and intelligence and later as the assistant chief of staff at the Headquarters, 62nd Troop Command. He served with distinction as the commander of the 3rd Battalion 200 Leadership Regiment; 167th Materiel Management Command; and the 621st Troop Support Command. Upon his promotion to brigadier general, he was assigned as the assistant adjutant general, Army Joint Forces Headquarters, Alabama Army National Guard.

BRIGADIER GENERAL REUBEN D. JONES

Former Commanding General, Family, Morale, Welfare and Recreation Command

Brigadier General Reuben Jones is one of the Army's newest two-star generals. Born in West Point, Mississippi, he graduated from Jackson State University in 1978 with a Bachelor of Arts degree in Sociology. He was commissioned through the ROTC program at Jackson State University. He also holds a Master of Strategic Studies degree from the Army War College and a Master of Arts degree in Administration from Central Michigan University. His military education includes the Adjutant General Basic Officer Course, the Adjutant General Officer Advanced Course, the Airborne School, the Military Personnel Officer Course, the Combined Arms Services Staff School, the Command and General Staff College, and the Army Senior Service College. Since graduation from Jackson State and being commissioned through the Army ROTC program, he has commanded soldiers across the world; from South Carolina, Indiana, Maryland and Virginia to Germany and Korea. Prior to reporting to the Family and Morale, Welfare and Recreation Command, Brig. Gen. Jones served as the adjutant general of the U.S. Army, Commanding General, U.S. Army Physical Disability Agency and executive director, Military Postal Service Agency, Alexandria, Virginia.

BRIGADIER GENERAL LLOYD MILES

Former Deputy Commanding General, I Corps and Fort Lewis

Brigadier General Miles' 30-year infantry career has taken him throughout the Army and around the world. America's Corps welcomed him to the newly established joint military base of the Army and Air Force during a ceremony in front of the I Corps Headquarters Building on August 5, 2010. Prior to his arrival, Brig. Gen. Miles was directly responsible for training the Iraqi Army. He had previously served as assistant commandant/deputy commanding general of the Infantry School and Center at Fort Benning.

He was commissioned as a second lieutenant in the Infantry from the Military Academy in 1980. His early assignments included duties in Germany, Egypt, and Kosovo. His military education includes: Airborne, Ranger, Pathfinder, Air Assault Schools, Infantry Officer Basic and Advanced Courses, Command and

General Staff College, the Joint Staff Officer Course, and a Master's degree in strategic studies from the Army War College. He holds a Bachelor of Science degree from the U.S. Military Academy.

BRIG. GEN. OWEN MONCONDUIT

First Black General Officer in Louisiana National Guard

On Feb. 17, 2009, Brig. Gen. Owen Monconduit was the first black officer in the Louisiana National Guard to be promoted to the rank of brigadier general. The commander of the 225th Engineer Brigade received his first star during a ceremony on Camp Liberty, Iraq.

Monconduit graduated from Louisiana State University in 1984 with a Bachelor of Engineer Technology, from the University of Phoenix in 1998 with a Master of Arts in Organizational Management, and from the United States Army War College in 2007 with a Master's in Strategic Studies. During his 28-year career, Monconduit served as a platoon leader, company executive officer, and as a company and battalion commander with the 225th Engineer Brigade. He became the chief of the environment management section for the Louisiana National Guard in 1991, where he served before becoming the Construction Management and Facilities officer in 2000. Before accepting command of the Engineer Brigade in 2007, Monconduit served as the executive officer to the adjutant general of the Louisiana National Guard, Maj. Gen. Bennett C. Landreneau.

A veteran of Operation Enduring Freedom, he commanded the 528th Engineer Battalion from Monroe, La., through a year-long tour to Afghanistan in 2005 before leading a battalion for six months on state-active duty for Hurricanes Katrina and Rita. Monconduit's awards include: the Bronze Star Medal, the Meritorious Service Medal, the Army Superior Unit Award, the Army Reserve Components Achievement Medal, the National Defense Service Medal, the Global War on Terrorism Expeditionary Medal, the Global War on Terrorism Service Medal, the Humanitarian Service Medal, and the Army Reserve Components Overseas Training Ribbon.

LIEUTENANT GENERAL JOHN W. MORGAN III

Former Commander Allied Force Command, Heidelberg

On May 5, 2010, Lieutenant General John Morgan assumed command of Allied Force Command, Heidelberg. The multinational NATO Headquarters, with an established strength of about 450 military personnel and civilians from 21 NATO nations and three partner nations, is symbolic of an enduring alliance that has defended democracy for over sixty years.

The command continues to enhance the capabilities of NATO in support of its operations in Afghanistan. Lt. Gen. Morgan previously served as the chief of staff, U.S. European Command; assistant chief of staff, United Nations Command, Combined Forces Command, United States Forces Korea; and deputy commanding general, Eighth United States Army. He was responsible for providing direction for all Republic of Korea and U. S. Forces assigned to the Korean peninsula. Lt. Gen. Morgan was commissioned as a field artillery officer at University of Delaware as a distinguished military graduate with a Bachelor of Science degree in Criminal Justice. He holds a Master of Science degree in National Security and Strategic Studies from the National Defense University.

MAJOR GENERAL DANA J. H. PITTARD

Former Commanding General, Fort Bliss, Texas

Major General Pittard assumed command of Fort Bliss—the largest military maneuver practice area behind the National Training Center—on July 9, 2010. Maj. Gen. Pittard was commissioned as a 2nd lieutenant from the U.S. Military Academy in 1981, with a Bachelor of Science degree in history. He later earned a Master's degree from the School for Advanced Military Studies at the Command and General Staff College. He attended the John F. Kennedy School of Government at Harvard University as a Senior Service College Fellow. Prior assignments include service as the deputy chief of staff, G-3/5/7 Army Training and Doctrine Command, and the commanding general of the National Training Center. More than 50,000 soldiers rotate through the National Training Center each year. Maj. Gen. Pittard took command in 2007. He previously served as the commander of Iraq Assistance Group from 2006 through June 2007; as a military aide to President Bill Clinton; and commander of 1-32 Armor/1-14 Cavalry at Fort Lewis as part of the Army's first Stryker Brigade.

BRIGADIER GENERAL BELINDA PINCKNEY

Former Director, Army Diversity Task Force

Brigadier General Pinckney is a member of the Finance Corps. She credits her elementary math school teacher for giving her a foundation and love for math. After she enlisted in 1976, she took advantage of every opportunity to advance up the chain of command. She has served as an Army element commander, Defense Finance and Accounting Service; military assistant, Assistant Secretary of the Army, Financial Management and Comptroller; and a budget analyst in the Technology Management Office, Office of the Chief of Staff. She was the first woman in the history of the Army Finance Corps to be promoted to a general officer and the first ever person to be nominated from the comptroller field. Her first major assignment was as deputy director, Defense Finance and Accounting Service, the largest finance and accounting operation in the world. When she took the reins of the U.S. Army Community and Family Support Center in 2006, she was the first woman and the first African-American to command the organization. Brig. Gen. Pinckney was appointed to head the Army's Diversity Task Force in 2007. She earned a Bachelor of Science degree in business administration at the University of Maryland, a Master of Public Administration degree in Financial Management at Golden State University, and a Master of Science degree in national resource strategy from the Industrial College of the Armed Forces.

GEN. COLIN L. POWELL

First Black Chairman of the Joint Chiefs of Staff

Born Colin Luther Powell on April 5, 1937, in Harlem, New York. Powell is the son of Jamaican immigrants Luther and Maud Powell. He was raised in the South Bronx and educated in the New York City public schools, where he graduated from Morris High School in 1954 without any definite plans for his future. It was at City College of New York, where Powell studied Geology, that he found his calling—in the Reserve Officers' Training Corps (ROTC). He soon became commander of his unit. This experience set him on a military career and gave him structure and direction in his life. After graduation in 1958, Powell was commissioned as a 2nd lieutenant in the U.S. Army. While stationed at Fort Devens, Massachusetts, Colin Powell met Alma Vivian Johnson of Birmingham, Alabama, and they married in 1962. The couple now has three children: a son named Michael, and daughters named Linda and Annemarie. That same year, he was one of 16,000 advisers sent to South Vietnam by President John Kennedy. In 1963, Powell was wounded by a punji-stick booby trap while patrolling the Vietnamese-Laotian border. During this first tour of duty, he was awarded a Purple Heart and, a year later, a Bronze Star.

While on his second Vietnam tour of duty from 1968 to 1969, the 31-year-old Army major was given the assignment of investigating the My Lai massacre. In this incident, more than 300 civilians were killed by U.S. Army forces. Colin Powell's report seemed to refute the allegations of wrongdoing and stated, "Relations between American soldiers and the Vietnamese people are excellent." Also during this tour in Vietnam, Powell was injured in a helicopter crash. Despite his injury, he managed to rescue his comrades from the burning helicopter, for which he was awarded the Soldier's Medal. In all, Powell has received eleven military decorations, including the Legion of Merit. Powell earned an MBA at George Washington University, in Washington, D.C., and won a White House fellowship in 1972. He was assigned to the Office of Management and Budget during the Nixon administration and made a lasting impression on Caspar Weinberger and Frank Carlucci. Both men would consult Powell for advice when they served as Secretary of Defense and national security adviser, respectively, in the Reagan administration. Colonel Colin Powell served a tour of duty in Korea in 1973 as a battalion commander and later obtained a staff job at the Pentagon. After studying at the Army War College, he was promoted to brigadier general and commanded a brigade of the 101st Airborne Division.

BRIGADIER GENERAL BRYAN T. ROBERTS

Former Commanding General, Fort Jackson, S.C.

Brigadier General Bryan T. Roberts assumed command of Fort Jackson April 10, 2012. He has served the Army for nearly 29 years in a variety of command and staff positions in the United States, Germany, Bosnia, and Iraq. A Distinguished Military Graduate of Eastern Michigan University, Brig. Gen. Roberts was commissioned as a second lieutenant of Armor in August 1983. He is a native of Hampton, Virginia. Just prior to taking command of Fort Jackson, he served in Operation New Dawn in Iraq as the Director, Iraq Training and Advisory Team—Army and Chief of Staff, Office of Security Cooperation –

Iraq. His other assignments include Fort Carson, Colorado; Schweinfurt, Germany; Bosnia, for Operation Joint Endeavor; Washington, D.C.; Fort Hood, Texas; New Orleans, during Hurricane Katrina Relief Operations; Iraq, during Operation Iraqi Freedom/Operation New Dawn, and Recruiting Command at Fort Knox, Kentucky. His awards and decorations include the Defense Superior Service Medal, the Legion of Merit, a Bronze Star Medal with Oak Leaf Cluster, a Defense Meritorious Service Medal with Oak Leaf Cluster, a Meritorious Service Medal with four Oak Leaf Clusters, an Army Commendation Medal with three Oak Leaf Clusters, a Joint Service Commendation Medal, an Army Achievement Medal, a Combat Action Badge, a Parachutist Badge and the Ranger Tab. He holds a Bachelor's degree in Commercial Marketing and Merchandising from Eastern Michigan University, a Master's degree in Administration from Central Michigan University, and a Master's degree in National Security Strategy and Strategic Studies from the National War College. Roberts is the 45th commanding general in Fort Jackson's 95-year history. Roberts and his wife, Cassandra, have two sons and one daughter.

GEN. ROSCOE ROBINSON, JR.

First black four-star general

Gen. Roscoe Robinson Jr. has had assignments ranging from U.S. representative to the North Atlantic Treaty Organization Military Committee, International Military Activities; Commanding General, 82nd Airborne Division, Fort Bragg, N.C.; Deputy Chief of Staff of Operations, U.S. States Army Europe and Seventh Army; and Commanding General, United States Army Japan/IX Corps. He retired from active duty on Nov. 30, 1985, and remained active in business, conducting several studies for the Army. He served as the chairman of the review panel to study the performance of the 24th Infantry Regiment during the Korean War. Attesting to his lifetime of service to the nation, the Association of Graduates of the USMA awarded him the Distinguished Graduate Award in May, 1993.

MAJOR GENERAL ABRAHAM J. TURNER

Former Chief of Staff, United States Strategic Command

Major General Turner earned his commissioning into the Army as an infantry officer through the ROTC at South Carolina State University in 1976 with a

Bachelor of Science Degree in Music. While attending the Army War College, he earned a Master's degree in Public Administration from Shippensburg University. Prior to his current assignment, Maj. Gen. Turner was deputy chief of staff, G-3/5/7, Army Training and Doctrine Command. His previous assignments include service as commanding general, Army Training Center and Fort Jackson; assistant chief of staff, C-3, Coalition Forces Land Component Command, Kuwait; assistant division commander, Fort Bragg; and chief, House Legislative Liaison Division, Office of the Chief, Legislative Liaison, U.S. Army, Washington, D.C.

LIEUTENANT GENERAL DENNIS L. VIA

Former Director, Command, Control, Communications & Computer (C4) Systems Directorate (J6) The Joint Staff

Lieutenant General Via was principal adviser to the chairman of the Joint Chiefs of Staff on all C4 systems matters within the Department of Defense. He was a luncheon speaker at MILCOM 2010, one of the largest government/industry networking and information-sharing events.

Lt. Gen. Via graduated in 1980. He began his career with the 35th Signal Brigade, XVIII Airborne Corps. Principal assignments include commanding general, Communications-Electronics Life Cycle Management Command, where he led an organization of over 10,000 military and civilian personnel responsible for coordinating, integrating, and synchronizing the life-cycle management of the command, control, communications, computers, intelligence, surveillance and reconnaissance systems for all of the army's battlefield areas.

GEN. WILLIAM E. (KIP) WARD

Former Commander of U.S. Army Africa Command (AFRICOM)

Gen. William E. (Kip) Ward became the first commander of U.S. Africa Command in Stuttgart, Germany, on Oct. 1, 2007. U.S. Africa Command is one of six unified geographic commands within the Department of Defense unified command structure. Ward was commissioned into the Infantry in June, 1971. His military education includes the Infantry Officer Basic and Advanced courses, U.S. Army Command and General Staff College, and the U.S. Army War College. He holds a Master's of Arts degree in Political Science from Penn State University and a Bachelor's of Arts degree in Political Science from Morgan

State University. His military service has included overseas tours in Korea, Egypt, Somalia, Bosnia, Israel, two tours in Germany, and a wide variety of assignments in the United States, including Alaska and Hawaii. Prior to assuming his current position, Ward was Deputy Commander, Headquarters U.S. European Command, Stuttgart, Germany. He previously served as the Deputy Commanding General/Chief of Staff, U.S. Army Europe and Seventh Army. While in this capacity, he was selected by the Secretary of State to serve as the United States Security Coordinator, Israel – Palestinian Authority, where he served from March through December 2005.

BRIGADIER GENERAL NADJA Y. WEST, M.D.

Former Commander, Europe Regional Medical Command

President Obama nominated Colonel West to be a brigadier general in April, 2010. She relinquished command of Womack Army Medical Center to take command of the Europe Regional Medical Command in Landstuhl, Germany. She had served as a physician at Fort Bragg since July, 2008. After graduating from the Military Academy with a Bachelor of Science in Engineering, she attended the George Washington University School of Medicine in Washington, D.C., where she earned her Doctorate of Medicine. She completed internship and residency in family practice at Martin Army Hospital. While on this assignment, she was deployed during Operation Desert Shield and was attached to 269th Armored Battalion. Dr. West completed a second residency in dermatology at Fitzsimons Army Medical Center and the University of Colorado Medical Center. She was then assigned as the chief, Dermatology Service at Heidelberg Army Hospital in Germany, and she served as the division surgeon of 1st Armored Division in Bad Kreuznach, Germany. She deployed to Macedonia and Kosovo as the deputy task force surgeon during this assignment. She was then assigned as chief, Department of Medicine and the Dermatology Service at the 121st General Hospital in Seoul, Korea. She graduated from the National War College, earning a Master's of Science in National Security Strategy. She was then assigned to the National Naval Medical Center at Bethesda as the Deputy Commander for Integration, becoming the first Army officer to join the leadership team at NNMC. She is a fellow of the American Academy of Dermatology and the American Academy of Family Practice.

BRIGADIER GENERAL LARRY D. WYCHE

As commanding general, Joint Munitions Lethality, Life Cycle Management Command/Joint Munitions Command, Brigadier General Wyche was named deputy chief of staff for logistics and operations, U. S. Army Materiel Command, Fort Belvoir, Va. Brig. Gen. Wyche was commissioned as a Quartermaster officer in 1983. Previous assignments include recent redeployment from Operation Enduring Freedom, Afghanistan, where he served as commander of the Joint Logistics Command, Combined Joint Task Force-76; commander, 4th Forward Support Battalion, 4th Infantry Division; logistics planner, and chief of readiness, Assistant Chief of Staff, Logistics, XVIII Airborne Corps.[6]

COL. CHARLES YOUNG

An unheralded military hero, Charles Young (1864-1922) was the third black graduate of West Point, the first African-American national park superintendent, the first black U.S. military attaché, the first African-American officer to command a Regular Army regiment, and the highest ranking black officer in the Regular Army until his death.

Part V
My Story: The Autobiography of My Life
(From Birth to Military Retirement)

My Humble Beginnings

I was born March 2, 1966 in a small country town called Franklin, Virginia. At the time of my birth, my mother was a school teacher in Boykins, Va and my father was an Airborne Paratrooper in the U.S. Army stationed at Fort Bragg, NC. For the first two years of my life, we lived in a small two-bedroom house in Boykins, my Mom's hometown. Boykins is a small town of less than one hundred people in Southampton County, at the junction of routes 35 and 186 near the North Carolina state line.

> *A little history trivia: In 1831, Southampton County was the location of the most serious slave rebellion in United States history. On August 21-22, the infamous Southampton Insurrection, led by the slave Nat Turner, resulted in the deaths of 58 whites and an unknown number of blacks. Turner and his followers were captured and tried, and twenty were hanged.*

Terrible Twos

The *terrible twos* is a term for the stage that toddlers go through that is categorized by temper tantrums, saying no to everything, or refusing to do as they are told. This described my behavior very well. I clearly remember when it started. My parents bought me a red tractor that I immediately got on and started playing with. Whenever they would make me take a break and come in the house, I would throw myself on the ground and flop back and forth like a fish on land. The temper tantrums eventually ended but it took many spankings to get me to that point. Since both of my parents worked, my oldest sister, Alveta, usually had to attend to me. She had full authority to discipline me and she would not hesitate to do so. Actually, our entire town had full authority to discipline me. The age-old saying is very true, it takes an entire village to raise a child.

The Big Move to the City

Portsmouth, Virginia traces its history to the plantation of Col. William Crawford, who laid out the boundaries of what became a city. As early as 1608, English explorers led by Capt. John Smith journeyed from the James River to the Elizabeth River and took note of a beautiful and bountiful area that would be later known as Portsmouth. African-Americans in Portsmouth built a strong, insulated community because they were cognizant of the need to look inward. Whether assisting the pre-Civil War escapes through the Underground Railroad, forming banks, publishing a newspaper, or providing recreational facilities, Portsmouth's African-Americans created one of the most stable middle-class black communities in America. My family relocated to Portsmouth when I was two years old.

Portsmouth is a city of twenty-nine square miles in the heart of Hampton Roads. With a population of 1.4 million, Hampton Roads is the nation's 27th latest metropolitan area. It is home to one of the largest military complexes in the world. Portsmouth is bordered by four neighboring cities, Chesapeake, Suffolk, Norfolk and Virginia Beach. Portsmouth is within 750 miles of two-thirds of the nation's population and industrial activity. A vibrant community on the shore of the Elizabeth River and a tidal arm of the Chesapeake Bay, its preservation of old-world influences and a rich nautical heritage give the city a unique an irresistible charm. With prime land yet to be developed, residential and commercial areas are thriving and growing. Continued growth and success are its future. A perfect combination of the old and the new is what continues to energize the city of Portsmouth.

Our first stop in Portsmouth was Hobson Street in the community of Truxton. Shortly after settling into our home in the Truxton section of Portsmouth, my family joined the Noble Street Baptist Church. My youngest sister, Michelle, was born February 6, 1969 at the Portsmouth Naval Hospital. Now I had a little sister. Cool, I was three at the time. I guess my parents planned it that way. I wasn't sure if they would have been able to handle my *terrible twos* and a newborn all at the same time. At the tender age of four, we moved across town to 719 Hancock Ave in the Cavalier Manor section of Portsmouth. Cavalier Manor was developed in the fall of 1943, during World War II because there was a critical shortage of housing for defense workers in the Norfolk Naval Shipyard and other government agencies in the area. Neighborhood Number 16, as it was called, began with the construction of Victory Manor, Cavalier Manor, and Lincoln Gardens. Gust Lane and Victory Boulevard bordered this area on the east, the Norfolk and Western Railroad on the south, Interstate 64 on the north, and the Portsmouth city line on the west.

We got settled in our new home just in time for me to start kindergarten. I attended kindergarten exactly three blocks from our new home. The late Reverend Harris was my kindergarten teacher. She was a tall, heavy-set lady who did not play around. She took her job very seriously. I'll never forget my first day of kindergarten. Within the first hour of arriving at school, I was leaning back in my chair (after being told not to) and fell. I busted my head and was taken to the emergency room where I received 8 stitches. What a way to start kindergarten. It got much better after that. I established some very good friendships. Many of them were friendships I would end up maintaining for many years. My best friend growing up, James Johnson, lived right around the corner from my family. He and I were the same age and his younger sister, Juanita, and Michelle were also the same age. James and I would walk to kindergarten every morning, in rain, sleet or snow.

Simonsdale Elementary School (1st and 2nd Grades)

In elementary school, I excelled in art, math, and science. I enjoyed drawing and won a few art contests. One drawing I won't forget was my portrait of the legendary John Henry Johnson. I won 1st place with that drawing. Just like most 1st graders, I was increasingly influenced by my peers, siblings, and television. Mrs. Trice was my 2nd grade teacher. She was a wonderful, tough, caring lady. I will never forget her and the many lessons she taught me. I will also never forget those many spankings I received with her 12-inch wooden ruler. She knew how to angle your hand so that the ruler would reach the thin tender portion of your palm instead of the thick meaty area. My upbringing at home was the key to success during my early school years. My parents taught me and my siblings the "4 Rs":

1. *Respect*. Even though most of my early friends were boys, I started to experience crushes on girls at a very early age. My parents taught

me to respect girls at an early age and this lesson has stuck with me throughout my life.

2. *Routines.* I had the benefit and responsibility of having an elementary school teacher as a mom. My mother incorporated a stable routine with me as early as 1st grade. There was a set time for playing out doors, taking a bath, cleaning, reading, and doing homework, with a little time allocated for watching TV. This was all part of my daily routine.

3. *Reassurance.* Some 1st graders can be hard on themselves when they make mistakes. My parents knew when to remind me of the progress I had made in the past year, from reading books to riding bikes to doing my chores. They also emphasized the need to explain my mistakes to me in a manner so that I could learn from them and grow.

4. *Rest.* Bedtime was bedtime and staying up late during the school week was not an option. My parents made sure I got my 8-10 hours of sleep every night.

My Adolescence Years

Children, be obedient to YOUR parents in union with [the] Lord, for this is righteous: "Honor your father and [your] mother"; which is the first command with a promise: "That it may go well with you and you may endure a long time on the earth." —Ephesians 6:1-3

Elementary School

As children grow they experience many biological, cognitive, and emotional changes. Along with these developments come changes in their social interactions with the world in which they live. In the toddler and early elementary years, children's social experiences are determined mostly by family and school contacts. That was exactly the case with me. My adolescent years were tough and exciting times, with many biological, cognitive, and social/emotional challenges. Life skills are all about having strong character and in general being a good person. Manners are a big part of life skills. My parents instilled them in me at a very early age. My siblings and I learned early to say *please* and *thank you*. I have carried that throughout my life and it has truly helped mold me into a better person.

Church

I had the fortune of learning these priceless life lessons not only at home but also within my church, school and local community. The saying "its take a village to raise a child" is very true. The church played a significant role in my spiritual and moral character development. The church my family attended was called the New First Baptist Church Taylorsville. History has it that in 1905, a revivalist from Charles City County named Reverend Evans organized the First Baptist Church Taylorsville and became its first pastor.

The church prospered over the decades under the leadership of several different pastors. By far, the longest tenured pastor was the late Reverend Thomas Melvin Steele, from Troy, North Carolina. Pastor Steele led the congregation faithfully for 45 years until his retirement in 2001. During his tenure, a new church was built and was called New First Baptist Church Taylorsville. I joined this church and accepted Christ when I was only seven years old. I remember it vividly, because our church revival was going on at the time and I had to sit in the very first pew until the service was over. The revival lasted late into the night and I found myself dozing off on a few occasions.

Growing Up in the 'Hood

Joining the church at an early age did not stop me from learning some of life's tough lessons that all kids go through. My best friend, James, and I enjoyed throwing things. We would throw footballs, baseballs, basketballs, and occasionally we would throw rocks. After awhile, we would get bored and start throwing rocks at cars. As we were playing in my front yard (at the intersection of Strafford Street and Hancock Ave) cars were always speeding by. So we decided one afternoon that we would get these vehicles to slow down by throwing rocks at them. Obviously, this was not a good idea and it nearly caused several accidents at that busy intersection. One driver swerved after having his car hit by our rocks. He pulled over, shouting obscenities at James and me. Fortunately for both of us, my parents were not home at the time, but my sister, Alveta, told them when they got home and of course, I received a spanking that night. On another occasion, James and I got bored and started throwing rocks at each other.

It started out with small pebbles and gradually moved up to larger rocks. Eventually, I didn't duck in time for one rock and got hit in the forehead. I needed eight stitches to close the gash. James and I both got spankings again. I could not understand why I was being punished when I was the one who got hit. Never again did I throw rocks at cars or people.

That was not to be my last incident requiring stitches. On one occasion, all the neighborhood boys were playing a game of baseball down the street from my house in the Williams' backyard. We were told many times about not to fling the bat after hitting the ball. Most of us understood the importance of not flinging the bat. However, on this sunny afternoon, Mike J (who lives around the corner from me), was at bat and I was playing catcher. He hit the ball, flung the bat and hit me in the corner of my eye socket. The blow almost put my eye out, and meant another eight stitches.

Earle's Supermarket

Earle's supermarket was located at the corner of Greenwood Drive and Victory Blvd. It was the only supermarket in our neighborhood and was about four blocks from home. My Mom would often take my sisters and me with her when she went grocery shopping. As I got a little older, James and I would often wander up to the store and buy candy with our allowance money. Once or twice when we didn't have any money, we would go to the store and steal candy. It became a big game for us. We would see how much candy we could stuff into our pockets. Eventually we got caught stealing candy one afternoon. The store manager detained us and called our parents. That night I received one of the worst spankings in my life. My Mom would spank me first and then sent me to my room. When Dad got home from work, he came into my room and gave me another whipping.

Dogs

My family loved dogs. Our first dog's name was Sparky. He was a small black dog. We kept him locked up in a dog kennel in our back yard. It was my responsibility to feed Sparky and keeping his dog pen clean. This is a chore that I did not look forward to, especially in the winter. We would occasionally let Sparky out of his pen so that he could run around in the yard. He loved that. It gave him the opportunity to release all of that built-up energy from being locked down for days at a time. My parents would not allow us to bring Sparky inside the house. This was okay in the summer and spring but our winters got pretty cold at times. One winter morning as I walked outside to feed Sparky, I quickly noticed that Sparky was not up and running around his pen. That was very unusual because he would always be excited when he saw me coming out with food. When I entered his pen, he still did not come out from his doghouse. As I looked into his doghouse, I could see that he was not moving. I touched him and he was cold as ice. He had frozen to death over night. The entire family was saddened by Sparky's death.

Cavalier Manor Recreation Department

Our neighborhood had one of the best recreation departments in the City of Portsmouth. We took youth sports very serious. The Tidewater area has long been known for producing some of the greatest athletes in the country. Michael Vick, Allen Iverson, Bruce Smith, J.R. Reid, Ronal Curry, E.J. Manuel and Alonzo Mourning are just a few of our local athletes who excelled in pro sports. Soccer was the first organized sport I participated in. Our neighborhood soccer league was extremely competitive. Parents took it just as serious as us kids. The hand, feet and eye coordination I learned in soccer would eventually become very valuable to me as I went on and excelled in other sports like football, wrestling and track. Our community recreation center offered a comprehensive swimming program, and I learned to swim at a young age.

The Bikes

One year, James and I both got bikes for Christmas. We would ride our bikes all over the neighborhood. One afternoon, we decided to stop at Earle's Supermarket and buy some candy. We both had bike chains and figured there was no harm in stopping at Earle's. We locked our bikes up behind the store and were inside for no more than fifteen minutes. When we returned to get our bikes, we were shocked to find out that someone had cut our bike locks and stolen our brand new bikes. Needless to say, that was the longest walk home, trying to figure out how to break the news to our parents. Not only did I get a spanking for being up at Earle's, where I wasn't supposed to be, but my parents refused to buy me another bike until they decided I had learned my lesson.

Matriculation from Elementary to Middle School

The initial transition from elementary school to middle school was extremely challenging for me, to say the least. Like all middle schoolers, I had to adjust to the onset of puberty along with experiencing a level of self-doubt, insecurity and confusion that didn't occur before. By the time I finished elementary school I was "the man" at my school. Everyone knew me; classmates, teachers, and principals. I was now moving on to middle school, where I was just one of many new guys. I also felt a new sense of insecurity fueled by a drive to stand out from the rest of the crowd and a need for positive affirmation. This led to fierce competition between the guys, who were all competing for girls, attention, sports, and grades.. We were constantly competing for attention from peers and at home. Although the difficult road of adolescence is the only route from childhood to maturity, having my parents there for me made all the difference. Middle school teachers are a rare breed. They were my heroes! To be a middle school teacher requires great patience and creativity, along with dedication and a great sense of humor.

Family Reunions

Family reunions were an instrumental part of both of my parents' families. My Mom's side of the family (the Persons) celebrated their family reunion during Homecoming Weekend, which is the first Sunday in August. Events were held in Branchville, Virginia and consisted of church services at Rising Star Baptist Church, dinners, cookouts, and family get-togethers. Many of the social events were coordinated and hosted by my late Aunt Irene's children. I always looked forward to returning to the country for Homecoming. It was a great chance to see my relatives and get caught up on old times. Afterward, many of us would head to Virginia Beach for a few days of fishing, swimming and hanging out. On my Dad's side of the family, the majority of the Sharpe-Bynum family reunions were held in Wilson, North Carolina, which is where my Dad's family grew up. The Wilson Chapel Church was always one of our focal points. Most of my Dad's relatives attended Wilson Chapel and the majority of the church members were close friends of the Sharpe family. Several of our family reunions were held at the Wilson Chapel Family Center. The traditional events included gospel singing (including the Wilson Chapel Male Chorus), talent shows, health fairs, and of course great home cooking. My Uncle Paul, who lived in Portsmouth and had a very large house and yard, would host some of the Family Reunions as well.

My Pre-Teen Years

Growing up in the 'hood, it's always been a heavy experience to turn back and look at the way we grew up. With or without parents, with all our struggles, all our emotions and those special friends, it's no wonder people sing about it all the time.

Playing Touch Football in the Street

Playing two-hand-touch football in the street was one of the favorite pasttimes for guys growing up in the Cavalier Manor section of Portsmouth. On any given afternoon, you could find multiple football games going on. We would try to find a section of the neighborhood where there was not a lot of traffic. The last thing we wanted to was to have to stop the game to let cars pass. The games grew more competitive as we got older. We took winning very seriously and we kept a running record of our wins and losses. For the most part, the injuries were minor but every once in a while someone would twist an ankle or bruise their leg. As we got old enough to try out for JV and Junior League tackle football, we gave up playing football in the streets to avoid any potential injuries.

Junior League Tackle Football

Most of the guys who grew up with me in Cavalier Manor wanted to try out for tackle football. However, most of us didn't have transportation to attend JV tryouts and practices at the local high school. There were no activity buses at that time and most of our parents worked. A few of the Cavalier Manor recreation center coordinators got together and formed a Junior League tackle football program for guys like me who were too old and too big for little league. They created four teams in the first year of the league. I was assigned to the Cavalier Manor Colts. My coach was a former college football star who knew the ins and outs of tackle football. He did a great job teaching us the basics (i.e., blocking, tackling, and running plays). We had a few great players too. Will, our star running back, could have easily starred at the varsity high school level. For whatever reason, he never got that chance to play in high school but he did help us win the Cavalier Manor Junior League Championship.

Church Involvement

By the time I was thirteen, my mother had gotten my sisters and I involved in most of the youth programs at the church. My oldest sister sang in the choir while my youngest sister and I served on the Junior Usher Board. We also were active in Sunday School, Youth Missionaries, and Vacation Bible School. During my junior year in high school, I was appointed Vice President of the Junior Usher Board. As the "Keepers of the Door," our mission was to help set the spiritual tone for learning and worshipping by greeting, seating, collecting the offering, maintaining order during service and attending to the special requests of the people.

Vacation Bible School

My mother also made sure that my siblings and I always participated in the church Summer Vacation Bible School. VBS is a summer evening event that includes Bible lessons, crafts, games, and singing. VBS affects not only the children but also their homes and communities.

W. E. Waters Junior High School: "Time to Get Organized"

"Education is the most powerful weapon which you can use to change the world" —Nelson Mandela.

History Trivia

W. E. Waters Junior High School was named after Mr. William Emerson Waters, who was a teacher and principal at I. C. Norcom High School. He was well known for his civic, social, and religious contributions to the city of Portsmouth. The building was opened in September 1966, including grades 6 through 9, with an enrollment of 800 students. It now has an enrollment of 765 students, a staff of 56 teachers, three administrators. a full-time nurse, three counselors, four secretaries, five cafeteria workers, and nine custodians. In 1969, Waters received its junior high school accreditation from the Southern Association of Colleges and Schools.

I attended W.E. Waters Junior High School, which was located six blocks from my home. My friends and I walked to school each morning. Mr. Vernon Randall was our Principal. Principal Randall was a firm but passionate man who loved helping and talking to kids. My junior high school reminded me of the movie *Lean on Me*. You did not want to have to go to Principal Randall's office. The outcome was usually not good, and in most cases it involved calling your parents. Reading, writing, and spelling skills were the cornerstones of our education at W.E. Waters. In addition, students were given broad exposure to literature in the form of short stories, novels, poetry and drama. I started to excel in math, art and science in junior high. I made the honor roll and was selected to the National Junior Honor Society. It was at this point that I started to get interested in engineering. Alcohol, drugs and teen pregnancy were constant problems in Portsmouth at the time. Peer pressure was always an issue. Guys and girls experimented with drugs and alcohol at young ages. This led to many bad decisions. Several of my junior high school classmates got pregnant even before they ever made it to high school.

The guys that I hung with were more of the preppy sports jocks. We experimented with a little beer from time to time and we would take a puff off a cigarette if the opportunity arose. But we were too scared of our parents to try anything more. During 8th grade, I would occasionally be late for school just so my Mom would have to take me. At that point, I would ask her to drive since it was only about six blocks away. That is how I got my first taste of driving. I eventually took drivers' education during my freshmen year.

W.E. Waters Junior High School Band

In the junior high band, membership was open to all students who wished to extend their knowledge, understanding, and appreciation of music by learning how to play an instrument. The only prerequisite was that you had to attend a grueling summer band camp. The worst part was the fact that we were in band camp during the hottest part of the summer while our friends were hanging at the beach and enjoying their summer. I tried out for 1st trumpet and made it. The competition was stiff and it meant hours of practice every night. I am pretty sure that my family grew tired of hearing me practice, even though they never really said so. But all the practice and sacrifice paid off when I was able to excel in our high school band and go on to make the I.C. Norcom High School Marching Band in my freshmen year.

My First Job: The Paper Boy

One of the many things that my parents stressed was the value of hard work and earning an honest day's pay. As soon as I turned twelve—which was the legal age to work at that time—I signed up for a local paper route with the *The Virginian-Pilot* and *Ledger-Star Newspaper Company*. I maintained my paper route for six years until I graduated from high school and went off to basic training. That paper route was my first job and it taught me a lot about discipline, finances, and communicating with adults. Every morning, I had to get up at 5 am, grab my grocery cart—which was posted in our backyard—and walk several blocks to pickup my stack of papers. My route averaged anywhere from 50-60 residents.

My Own Lawn Cutting Business

I considered myself to be somewhat of a young entrepreneur. In addition to having my own paper route, I also started my own lawn cutting business. It was a wise choice. The job was busiest when school was out, the hours were flexible, and the pay was good. My Dad helped me get the necessary equipment, which included a lawn mower, trimmer, and gasoline can. I advertised my business through word of mouth. Since I already had over sixty newspaper customers, it was easy to get the word out about my lawn cutting business. I maintained a large clientele for many years by having competitive prices and maintaining customer satisfaction by doing the job right every time.

Helping my Dad and Uncle at their Upholstery Shop

On some weekends, I would go to work at my Dad and Uncle's upholstery shop. Sharpe's Upholstery was located on Portsmouth Blvd across from the old Fork Union Military Academy. My Dad and uncle were both experts at reupholstering furniture pieces, like couches, chairs, ottomans, and sofas. They were also great at recovering car and boat seats along with making furniture slipcovers. I've seen them take old furniture that people had tossed out on the street and make it look new in less than a day. It was like magic watching them work.

The most important thing I learned from helping them out in the shop was that no matter how much experience you have or what tools you have, your customer shouldn't have to see the job until it's done right. For example, there's no way to earn while you learn in plumbing. If you have to go to a customer's house three times to fix a leaky pipe, they probably won't call you again. On the other hand, if you have to redo a seat deck, perhaps because you made a bad cut that shows, your client won't even know. You'll have a customer for life and they'll tell their friends.

My Dad and Uncle established a lasting reputation in Portsmouth for providing excellent service at a fair price. I had often considered going into the upholstery business myself but my talents and desires took me in another direction. But I made it a point to continue the Sharpe legacy of fine service at a fair price no matter what career I chose.

The "Big Divide" (Graduating from Junior High and Moving on to High School)

Me and most of the homies I grew up with all attended the same schools from 1st through 8th grade. We had established a strong bond over the years, even through all the fights and arguments. The good times clearly outweighted the bad. When it was time to graduate from junior high school, we all had major decisions to make. Growing up in Cavalier Manor, we had two options for high school. We could go to Manor High School, which was the newer and more modern choice. It was also less than six miles from our neighborhood. The other option was to get bused across town to I.C. Norcom High School, which was a vocational/college preparatory school. As we approached the end of 8th grade, this choice grew bigger and bigger. To make my decision even harder, my oldest sister, Alveta, had graduated from Manor just five years earlier in one of their first graduating classes. She established a strong academic record, graduating in three years and earning an academic scholarship to Virginia Commonwealth University. The academic standard had been set for me and my younger sister.

My High School Years

The process of transitioning from junior high to high school is one of the many developmental challenges that students face in adolescence. In addition to academic demands, beginning high school students often become distracted by the increased complexity of social interactions that are fostered within the high school environment. Peers emphasize fitting in and belonging, and this can be a great source of pressure and anxiety for many students. In addition, students who were top scholars and athletes in junior high school may experience role loss when they arrive in high school. I faced all of these challenges and more after graduating from W.E. Waters. But I had the distinct pleasure of attending one of the premier high schools in the Commonwealth of Virginia.

History Trivia: The History of I.C. Norcom High School

The Chestnut Street School was renamed I. C. Norcom in 1953 in honor of its first supervising principal, Israel Charles Norcom. The multi-faceted Mr. Norcom was described as a pioneer educator, leader of his people, churchman, civic leader, businessman, fraternalist, guidance counselor, and an outstanding citizen. Israel Charles Norcom, was born in Edenton, North Carolina on September 21st, 1856, one of John and Lucy Norcom's ten children. He attended school in North Carolina. He studied at Yale and Harvard Universities. After teaching for two years in Bedford County, Virginia, Israel Norcom became both teacher and principal at the Chestnut Street School (built in 1878), the precursor of I. C. Norcom High School. He served there from 1883 until 1916, the year of his death.

Freshman Year

My freshmen year started out with a bang. I spent the summer of 1981 auditioning and training as 1st trumpet player with the legendary I.C. Norcom High School Marching Band. We participated in several competitions, parades, and varsity football games. Of course, homecoming was always special, as we performed at halftime in front of a capacity crowd at Frank D. Lawrence Stadium in downtown Portsmouth. In addition to band, I decided to try out for the wrestling team. I have played a lot of sports in my life but I must admit that amateur wrestling is one of the toughest and most challenging sports there is. Everyday your stamina, will and intestinal fortitude are tested.

Drafting and Design Curriculum

Mr. Nixon was our Drafting and Design instructor. We got to know him very well because of the amount of time we spent in his room over the course of four years. Our design classes were two hours long, Monday through Friday. This was a very demanding but rewarding technical trade I grew to love. It required a lot of math and science with a splash of art. The students in this course became very good friends over the years because we spent so much time together in Mr. Nixon's class. Our high school curriculum was one of the most demanding technical trades at our high school. I spent many hours preparing drawings, making model buildings, developing blueprints and preparing presentations. However, for those who stuck it out over the entire four years, there was a great reward at the end. Most of us eventually headed off to some sort of architectural engineering or design major in college.

The Executives, Omega Kappa Psi Fraternity

In the early 1980s, high school fraternities and sororities were becoming very popular in local high schools. At my high school alone, there were over eight active fraternities and sororities. During my sophomore year I joined the Executives, which happened to be the unofficial "Little Brothers" to the Omega Psi Phi College fraternity. We got to know many of the Omegas at Norfolk State University (Pi Gamma Chapter). We attended some of their mentoring and sporting events and became their protégés. At I.C. Norcom High School, we were considered one of the premier organizations at the school. We sang in the halls, conducted community service projects, stepped in the local stepshow competitions, and conducted numerous fundraisers. We had our own fraternity sweaters, jackets and hats which all contained our symbols and logos. Most of our members were either in the band or played varsity sports. We were all about being good young Americans making a difference in our schools, communities, at church, and within our families. We strived to be young role models for the younger generation.

Fighting

Fighting was the thing to do in the late '70s and early '80s. The average high school student did not have access to guns and knives. The biggest rivalry was between P-town and Norfolk. Even though the two cities are only separated by a tunnel and bridge, there was no love lost between the guys who lived in Norfolk and my homies in Portsmouth. Not sure about the history behind all of this beef, but tensions were at an all-time high during the early '80s. Girls and sports rivalry were a big part of the drama. I.C. Norcom High School vs. Booker T. Washington High was a heated rivalry that dated back for decades. These were two of the premier mostly black high schools in the state of Virginia. Both schools had a strong reputation, especially when it came to athletics. There was almost guaranteed to be a fight either before, during, or after any sporting event between the two schools.

During my junior year at Norcom, we played an away game at Booker T. Washington. The game was very competitive and the referees did a good job of keeping things under control during the football game. The halftime performance was absolutely amazing. Both marching bands put on a show for the ages. Just as many people came to see the halftime show as those who came to see the game. I.C. Norcom would eventually win the football game. At the end of the game, as both teams were leaving the field, a fight broke out involving over a dozen players from both teams. The coaches were eventually able to break up the fight and get the players off the field. However, as our activity bus was leaving the stadium, several hostile fans started throwing rocks at our bus. Several windows were broken but, fortunately, no one was seriously injured.

Pre-Engineer Course Work

I made the decision to go to college and become an architectural engineer during my sophomore year. My love for art and drawing combined with my enrollment in the Drafting and Design vocational program, lead me to that decision. Now I had to add the math and science courses that were prerequisites for most engineering programs. I needed to take Pre-Calculus, Calculus, Trigonometry, and Biology. Coach Harner, my assistant wrestling coach, was our Biology teacher. He was an easygoing, down-to-earth guy, but he really made me earn my B in his class. I was like, "Hey Coach, you gonna actually make me dissect this frog". And the answer was always yes, with a smile on his face.

Varsity Sports

At the end of my freshmen year, I made the decision to give up band and focus on academics and sports. I made the varsity football team my sophomore year and we won the Southeastern District championship that year. We narrowly lost to First Colonial in the Eastern Regional Playoffs. It was a very emotional loss because our goal was to win the state championship. Our head coach, the late Joe Langston, and head assistant coach, Mr. Herman Terry, had assembled one of the strongest and deepest teams in decades. However, as fate had it, that was the closest we ever got to winning the Eastern Regional. My high school had several football rivalries but the Big 3, which were Manor, Wilson and Booker T. Washington. Regardless of who won those games, there was always a fight after the game.

For my junior year, I decided to add another sport. I tried out and made the boys' varsity track team. Coach Langston was also the track coach. He saw some track potential in me during football practices and recommended that I give track a try. I took him up on the offer and ended up lettering my first year on the team. We won the Southeastern District track meet each year I was at Norcom. Coach Langston had an amazing record as the I.C. Norcom track coach. His championships and awards are too numerous to count. His records have never been broken and probably never will.

I was now playing sports year-round. I started with football in the fall, and then wrestling in the winter, followed by track in the spring. The only way my parents allowed me to do this was if I maintained at least a "B" average. In addition to my parents and siblings, my coaches, athletic directors, and teachers all had a moral obligation to protect me and my fellow high school athletes, promoting better academics and education. Our high school was known for producing great athletes, scholars and citizens.

My senior year was great. We had one of the most outstanding senior classes. Our teachers would tell us that all the time. My senior class produced a record number of doctors, lawyers, engineers, architects, teachers, military veterans, and business owners, to name a few. The instructions and knowledge that we obtained during our high school days was priceless. I am forever graceful to my teachers, counselors, tutors and coaches. The memories are too many to discuss them all. Homecoming dance, junior and senior prom, our senior trip to Florida, dating, and being voted "friendliest" male—some girls would call it flirting but that's another whole story.

I capped my high school career off with a Southeastern District Varsity wrestling championship in the 145-pound weight class, followed by a Southeastern District Track championship in the spring of 1984. During this time, I also got the official word that I had been accepted to North Carolina A&T State University. It was the school I dreamed about attending.

Senior Trip to Walt Disney World Florida

My senior classmates and I had spent years working hard in school and now we were finally about to graduate. But before we graduated, we felt as though we deserved a senior class trip like no other class before us. One of the many signature events during my senior year was our senior class trip to Walt Disney World in Florida. I saved for months just to attend. My parents helped me as well. It was a once-in-a-lifetime moment. We had a pretty wild senior class and most of the folks that traveled on our senior trip went to party and have a good time. The bus driver/tour guide was a real cool older guy. He took care of us during the entire trip, including purchasing beer for us since we were all under-aged. We had several parties in our hotel rooms. We also went on several tours and hung out at the Disney Park and Epcot Center. Our Disney senior class trip was definitely a once-in-a-lifetime experience and we will cherish those memories for life.

Senior Prom

My senior prom was yet another great event that helped commemorate the end of high school. I took my high school sweetheart (VV) to the prom. She was a junior at one of our arch rivals, Wilson High School, but she still managed to have a great time. My Dad let me use his car, which was a gold Chevy Monte Carlo with mag rims. I washed and waxed the car the day before to ensure that it was ready for the occasion. Our parents took lots of pictures as she was decked out in a pink evening gown while I sported a white tuxedo. The food was great and the deejay did an outstanding job of entertaining the entire audience. We danced the night away. After the prom was over, we changed clothes and headed to an after-party at a hotel in Virginia Beach. It was a great weekend.

High School Graduation : The Class of 1984

This was a bittersweet time for me and my classmates. Many of us had been friends since kindergarten and elementary school. We had been through many highs and lows over the years. The reality was now setting in that we were about to graduate and move on with our lives. Our graduation class had accomplished so much over the past four years. The vast majority of our senior class received some sort of college scholarship. Some were awarded athletic scholarships in football, track, wrestling, basketball or baseball. Others received academic scholarships to many of the most prestigious colleges in the country. We had set the bar very high for the next group of senior classes. I received a partial track scholarship to North Carolina A & T State and was also accepted into their prestigious school of engineering program. In all, 1984 was a great year. As I think back and reminisce on many of the things that were going on at that time:

- World Series Champions: Detroit Tigers
- Super Bowl Champions: Los Angeles Raiders
- NBA Champions: Boston Celtics
- Stanley Cup Champs: Edmonton Oilers
- U.S. Open Golf: Fuzzy Zoeller
- U.S. Tennis: John McEnroe/Martina Navratilova
- Wimbledon (Men/Women): John McEnroe/Martina Naratilova
- NCAA Football Champions: BYU
- NCAA Basketball: Georgetown

Other Facts (1984)

- Singer Marvin Gaye (April 2, 1939-April 1, 1984) was shot and killed by his father on the day before his 45th birthday. God bless his soul.
- The Cosby Show debuted on NBC. The sitcom is widely considered the most popular show of the 1980s.
- Michael Dell started selling Dell Computers, targeting small businesses and households instead of the high-end consumers like his competitors (IBM, Apple, and Compaq).
- Prince and The Revolution and released the album *Purple Rain.*
- Vanessa Williams, the first African-American to win the Miss America title, was forced to give up her crown ten months later when nude photos of her were sold to Penthouse.
- Most Popular Christmas Gifts: Cabbage Patch Kids, Trivial Pursuit (specialty editions), Transformers.

The Summer of 1984

Shortly after graduation, my family and friends gave me a graduation/going-away party. A week later, I was on my way to Fort Leonard Wood, Missouri to attend Army Basic Training. Since I had joined the Army Reserves under the split-option program, I attended basic training during the summer of '84 and AIT during the summer of '85. This allowed me to enroll in college on time without missing any classes.

Basic Training

United States Army Basic Training is the program of physical and mental training required in order for an individual to become a soldier in the United States Army, United States Army Reserve, or Army National Guard. Basic Training is designed to be highly intense and challenging. The challenge comes as much from the difficulty of physical training as it does from the required quick psychological adjustment to an unfamiliar way of life. For me, it was my first time away from home. I did not have Mom and Dad to wake me up and make sure I was where I was supposed to be. Coming out of P-town, I thought I was as tough, smart and athletic as they come. I was sure basic training thing would be a piece of cake.

However, my drill instructors had a different view on things. They broke us down and rebuilt us into a cohesive team. They taught us the fundamentals of being a soldier, from combat techniques to the proper way to address a superior. We also underwent rigorous physical training to prepare our bodies and minds for the physical and mental strain of combat. One of the most difficult and essential lessons I learned was self-discipline. This was through my introduction to a strict daily schedule that entailed many duties and high expectations. It was a challenge I accepted and conquered. I graduated from basic training with honors. I can truly say that the summer of 1984 was when I grew up and started becoming a man.

IF—
by Rudyard Kipling

If you can keep your head when all about you
  Are losing theirs and blaming it on you,
If you can trust yourself when all men doubt you,
  But make allowance for their doubting too;
If you can wait and not be tired by waiting,
  Or being lied about, don't deal in lies,
Or being hated, don't give way to hating,
  And yet don't look too good, nor talk too wise:
If you can dream—and not make dreams your master;
  If you can think—and not make thoughts your aim;
If you can meet with Triumph and Disaster
  And treat those two impostors just the same;
If you can bear to hear the truth you've spoken
  Twisted by knaves to make a trap for fools,
Or watch the things you gave your life to, broken,
  And stoop and build 'em up with worn-out tools:
If you can make one heap of all your winnings
  And risk it on one turn of pitch-and-toss,
And lose, and start again at your beginnings
  And never breathe a word about your loss;
If you can force your heart and nerve and sinew
  To serve your turn long after they are gone,
And so hold on when there is nothing in you
  Except the Will which says to them: 'Hold on!'
If you can talk with crowds and keep your virtue,
  Or walk with Kings—nor lose the common touch,
If neither foes nor loving friends can hurt you,
  If all men count with you, but none too much;
If you can fill the unforgiving minute
  With sixty seconds' worth of distance run,
Yours is the Earth and everything that's in it,
  And—which is more—you'll be a Man, my son!

History Trivia

North Carolina Agricultural and Technical State University is a public, doctoral/research land-grant university committed to exemplary teaching and learning, scholarly and creative research, and effective engagement and public service. The university offers degrees at the baccalaureate, master's and doctoral levels and has a commitment to excellence in a comprehensive range of academic disciplines. This unique legacy and educational philosophy provide students with a broad range of experiences that foster transformation and leadership for a dynamic and global society. In 1890, Congress enacted the Second Morrill Act that mandated "a separate college for the colored race." The Agricultural and Mechanical College for the Colored Race (now N.C. A&T) was established as that school in the state of North Carolina by an act of the General Assembly ratified on March 9, 1891. Originally operating in Raleigh as an annex to Shaw University, the college made a permanent home in Greensboro with the help of citizens such as Dr. DeWitt (a black dentist), C. Benbow, and Charles H. Moore. In 1915, state legislators changed the college's name to the Agricultural and Technical College of North Carolina; and in 1967, they elevated it to university status. N.C. A&T became a constituent university of the University of North Carolina in 1972.

I must admit that my high school training had prepared me well for college. At least I was prepared academically. The social aspects, however, were a totally different thing. "A&T" had a reputation as a party school, and my first semester was no exception.

My Freshman Experience

Scott Hall was the freshman male dormitory. It was also the largest, loudest, and wildest dormitory on campus. It was like the movie *Animal House*. You could find "anything and everything" in Scott Hall, including sex, drug, alcohol, fights, card games, dominos and on some occasions, even studying took place). It was not really conductive to studying, to say the least. I normally had to complete my studying and homework before I returned to my dorm room. I attempted to maintain a long distance relationship with my high school sweetheart (VV).

She was a senior in high school and I was a freshman in college. I was exposed to more in my first two college semesters than I had been during my entire four years of high school. Needless to say, our long distance relationship did not last past my first semester. We were too young at the time to make it work. Having just completed basic training, I decided to give Army ROTC a try. It turned out to be one of the best decisions of my life. The Army training that I received during Basic made things fairly easy for me during my first year in ROTC. I excelled both academically and physically. Unbeknownst to me, I had selected one of the hardest and longest academic curricula to pursue—Architectural Engineering. It was one of the few official five-year majors at the time. Many curricula start out as four years and end up as five, but Architectural Engineering started out as five years and students went from there. My freshmen year went fairly smooth academically. I was able to make the dean's list with a 3.2 GPA. Things were going well and I could not have imagined a better start to college.

Summer of '85 in San Antonio, Texas

I spent the Summer of '85 attending Advanced Individual Training (AIT) at Fort Sam Houston in San Antonio, Texas. As a Combat Medic (MOS - 91A), I received extensive medical training that summer. I learned how to administer IVs, draw blood, and perform CPR, just to name a few of the tasks. It was a very competitive and intense environment. On average, 25% of the students did not graduate from this course. Many of them got recycled (which meant redoing that portion of the course before proceeding any further). I did the required studying and homework in order to pass the course. However, I still found time to do some sight-seeing and partying. The River Walk downtown was one of my favorite attractions. I was only nineteen at the time, which meant I wasn't old enough to get into the local clubs and bars. Me and my buddies—which is what those of us attending the combat medic course called ourselves—would rent a hotel room on the weekends and find someone who was 21 to have them buy us some beer. We threw several hotel room parties that summer in San Antonio, full of music, beer, girls, guys, food.

Upper Sophomore Year

Once I completed my AIT, I was fully qualified as a combat medic. I was assigned to a reserve hospital unit in Norfolk, about fifteen minutes from my parents' house in Portsmouth. Once a month, I had to catch a Greyhound bus or bum a ride home with one of my classmates in order for me to attend my monthly weekend drill. I eventually purchased my first car. It was a two-door metallic silver coupe. It looked much better than it drove. I also moved off-campus my sophomore year. I rented a room from a lady who owned a large boarding house minutes from campus. Things were going well until I started bringing girls home. There was nothing in my rental contract that mentioned company, so I didn't see anything wrong with it. But the landlord had a young kid and didn't think this was appropriate.

After that semester, I found a room at another house. I also decided to transfer from the hospital unit in Virginia to the 312th EVAC Hospital Unit just outside Greensboro. This made things much easier for me to attend drills. My cousin Ray was also a classmate and co-worker of mine. He had a nice Camaro that we would cruise around town in. I enjoyed my freshmen year in ROTC so much that I decided to apply for a three-year full ROTC scholarship. Three-year scholarships were available for students already enrolled in a college or university with three academic years remaining. I met all the requirements: I had U.S. citizenship, I was between the ages of 17 and 26, had high school GPA of at least 2.50 and minimum SAT score of 920. I applied and won the scholarship, which covered full tuition, room and board. This was such a great relief for my parents and me because we were paying out-of-state tuition and the partial track scholarship didn't cover much. I eventually gave up track and focused on engineering and ROTC. This was another one of the better decisions that I made in college. Part of my scholarship obligation was that I had to agree to accept a commission and serve in the Army on active duty for six years.

Pledging Omega Psi Phi Fraternity

January 1986 was a month that forever changed my life. I was invited to attend a smoker/interest meeting for one of the most powerful organizations on campus (or in the world for that matter). The Mu Psi Chapter of Omega Psi Phi Fraternity was about to start a line—called a pledge process—and I badly wanted to be part of it.

History Trivia

Omega Psi Phi Fraternity, Inc. is the first international fraternal organization to be founded on the campus of a historically black college. Omega Psi Phi was founded on November 17, 1911, at Howard University in Washington, D.C. The founders were three Howard University undergraduates, — Edgar Amos Love, Oscar James Cooper and Frank Coleman. Joining them was their faculty adviser, Dr. Ernest Everett Just.

When I arrived at A&T in the fall of 1984, the Ques were suspended. It turned out they had been suspended the entire time I had been at A&T up until now. Rumors started circulating during the fall of '85 that the Ques may be getting back *on the yard* in the spring of 1986. I made contact with a few of the Omegas and expressed my desire to become a part of the Omega Psi Phi fraternity. I eventually ran into a group of guys who were also trying to *make line* or join the fraternity. From January until mid-February 1986, we went around and visited other members of the fraternity to convince them that we were serious about wanting to become Omega Men. Over the weeks, the group of guys I had been hanging with started to become close friends. We got to know a lot about each others' pasts, families, goals and ambitions. When it was all said and done, fourteen of us—out of over 200 guys who attended the smoker/ interest meeting—made line. We felt like we had won the lottery.

But the hardest part was still ahead. The Bloody Mu Psi Chapter has been known for decades to be one of the hardest pledging chapters in the entire fraternity. Our official pledge process was about to start and my thirteen line brothers and I had no idea what we had gotten ourselves into. Before we knew it, Ques from all over the east coast were traveling to Greensboro to see the Mu Psi "lamps". We studied our material and practiced our routines for hours every night. We took pride in being thorough "lamps". Needless to say, our pledge period was extremely intense and rigid. We learned a lot about Omega Psi Phi, about the Mu Psi chapter, about each other, about life, and about ourselves. The poems we were required to memorize and recite are exactly what got us through those tough lonely dark nights in the *hole* on Plot Street.

We crossed the "burning sands" on March 27, 1986, which was the anniversary of our chapter's founding. That weekend was one of the highest and lowest points of my life. I had just successfully pledged the greatest fraternity in the world, but that very weekend we got the news that the chapter was being investigated for alleged hazing incidents. After a lengthy investigation, the chapter was suspended, which meant that we were not allowed to operate on campus as a student organization. My line brothers and I were crushed. We had gone through so much to get the opportunity to proudly serve our fraternity on campus, only to have that opportunity snatched from us. The suspension was tough on everyone—the school, the parents, the Chapter, my LBs, who were injured, our chapter advisors, and their families. My LBs and I felt as though we were victimized twice, by the fraternity during the pledge process and the school administration afterward. My LBs and I persevered and saw it through to the end. The poems we learned while pledging definitely became handy during our three-year suspension.

The Summer of 1986

The summer of 1986 was a busy and exciting summer. After completing the spring semester, I returned home to Portsmouth to work and take a few summer classes at Old Dominion University. I was able to get a job at Gwaltney Food Processing Plant shortly I arriving home doing assembly line work. A couple of my frat brothers and I worked the same shift, so we tried to make the job as fun as possible. We were always scheming to meet the finest women on our shifts. We got a reputation for being the new party college boys, who were just home for the summer. In some cases, it worked to our advantage and in other cases, the serious women chose not to waste their time.

One of the highlights of the summer was the Omega Psi Phi 75th Anniversary *Grand Conclave*. This historical event was held in Washington, D.C. in July of 1986. What made this event even more exciting was the fact that D.C. was where our fraternity was founded. Now as a neo (a new member in the Frat), I was actually about to take part in this history-making event. Several of my P-town homies pledged Omega during the spring of 1986. P-town has representation at St Paul's College, Virginia State, Norfolk State, the University of Wisconsin and, of course, North Carolina A & T State. Several of my *Sands* got together and road-tripped to D.C. for the Conclave. My Sands at Virginia State (Nu Psi Chapter) were participating in the Stepshow Championship and we were all rooting for them to win, which they eventually did. We partied and met brothers from all over the U.S. It was a beautiful week. Later that summer, I hung out with my brothers on most weekends. I took two classes at ODU and spent as much time in Virginia Beach as my schedule allowed. *"Omega by the Sea"* was the final event for the summer. It was a big beach party at Virginia Beach during Labor Day weekend. Ques from all over would come to Virginia Beach in order to spend one final weekend on the water.

Lower Sophomore Year

When I arrived on campus for my 3rd year, which we called Lower Sophomore Year, I had a different swag to my step. I had purchased a new black Escort GT. It was a sweet ride and I loved driving it. My Line Brother Zeke and I decided to rent an apartment. I applied for a job at UPS, which just happened to be one of the best paying jobs for college students. Life was good. Even though my fraternity was suspended, we still did a lot of things in the community and on campus. I was nominated for the NC A&T student senate and served with them for two years. As Omegas, we threw fundraising events at the Greensboro Depot, which was an old train station that had been converted into a club. People from all over the Greensboro area—including students at A&T, UNCG, Bennett, and Guilford Tech—came out to the Depot to party with us.

Homecoming was always an exciting time too. This would be my Line's first homecoming as members of the fraternity and we were very excited. We practiced for weeks to get our stepshow routine ready. We wanted to make sure that the older brothers accepted us and would be proud of us. We got permission from the Dean of Student Affairs to utilize our plot during homecoming, even though we were still officially suspended. Homecoming was a huge success.

Dating in College

Dating in college was very interesting, especially for the Omegas. We had a reputation for being wild and crazy. We were known for dating numerous girls, often at the same time. This made finding a nice steady girlfriend somewhat difficult, but I was up for the challenge. I found a little time in between working, ROTC, engineering classes, and the fraternity, to date on a semi-regular basis. Many of my LBs chose to date the Deltas. Greensboro had a lot of Deltas. A&T, UNC-Greensboro, and Bennett College all boasted Delta Sigma Theta chapters. I was friends with so many Deltas that it was in my best interest not to date any of them. I choose to date girls who didn't attend A&T initially. This kept the on-campus confusion down and minimized the chances of me getting busted.

The Pace Warehouse Embezzlement Scandal

Things were tight financially for most college students. I was going to school full-time while working part-time at UPS. I had to pay rent, car note, utilities and groceries. My house-mate and I survived mostly off hook-ups, just like many other college students. We had friends who worked at various fast food restaurants, grocery stores and other places. We would go through the drive-thru and get ten times more than what we paid for. Many times, we would take the extra food – especially the fried chicken – back to the dorms and sell it to our fellow dormmates. As time went on, the hook-ups gradually grew bigger.

We eventually ran across a friend of ours who worked at Pace Warehouse as a cashier. Pace Warehouse was a huge department store that sold everything from food to clothes to audio equipment. We would take leather jackets, jeans, shirts, watches, and food up to the cashier and she would only charge us a nominal amount. This was the serious hook-up, and the word was spreading all over campus and even to other local colleges. Needless to say, the store management eventually started getting suspicious as their inventory continued to dwindle. A larger investigation was launched and our friend, who happened to be dating my housemate, was caught hooking someone up at the cash register. Security monitored her for weeks and eventually my housemate and I were caught on camera getting the hook-up. A few days later, local police along and private detectives surrounded our apartment and we were both taken to jail. Luckily for us, it was our first offense and our lawyer was able to get us off on the first-time offender's program. We both had to do community service and stay out of trouble from then on.

This was definitely a wake-up call. I almost went to prison for embezzlement and almost lost my Army ROTC scholarship. It was extremely embarrassing to my family, co-workers, classmates and friends.

Upper Junior Year: Summer Advanced ROTC Camp '87

My spent the summer of 1987 completing the Army Advanced ROTC Camp at Fort Bragg, followed by Airborne School at Fort Benning, Georgia. ROTC Advanced Camp was a summer leadership camp where I learned advanced military tactics and gained experience in team organization, planning and decision-making. Entering the Advanced Course required a commitment to serve as an Officer in the U.S. Army after you graduate. Since I had already incurred a six-year active duty obligation with my ROTC scholarship, this was a given. My prior basic and AIT training made this summer camp much easier. That was not the case with all the ROTC Cadets who attended camp. Over 20% didn't graduate from camp. I performed well in all of my leadership positions and finished within the top 10% of our graduation class. I also got a chance to meet some very interesting people from all over the East Coast.

Of course, the Ques had a fairly large contingent of Cadets at Advanced Camp. I hung out with the Ques from all over the United States. I learned a lot about Omega Psi Phi, about the U.S. Army, and about life in general. More than anything, I learned a lot about myself. U.S. Army Airborne School, widely known as Jump School, conducts the basic paratrooper (military parachutist) training for the United States Armed Forces. It is operated by the 1st Battalion (Airborne), 507th Infantry, United States Army Infantry School, Fort Benning. The Airborne School conducts the Basic Airborne Course, which is open to troops of both genders from all branches of the United States Department of Defense and allied military personnel. The purpose of the Basic Airborne Course is to qualify the student in the use of the parachute as a means of combat deployment and to develop leadership, self-confidence, and an aggressive spirit through mental and physical conditioning. All students must volunteer to attend the course and may elect to quit at any time. The course is three weeks long and consists of three phases: "Ground Week", "Tower Week" and "Jump Week". Rigorous physical training (PT) is emphasized throughout the entire course. I was well-prepared for the physical portion of this course, but there was nothing that could have prepared me for jumping out of C130. Once it was over, we all felt great about it, but we were scared during the actual airborne operation. I was fortunate to have completed the course without any injuries.

Smoketree Apartments on Yanceyville Street

When I returned to A&T for the fall '87 semester, my housemate and I decided to move up in the world. We rented a two-bedroom apartment in the Smoketree Apartments off Yanceyville Street. These were some of the better apartment complexes in Greensboro and we had been on the waiting list for a year. The complexes included tennis courts, basketball courts, and private parking. All utilities were included in the rent. We really enjoyed staying in this complex. We stayed next door to two fine AKA sorority girls. There was never a dull moment between the two apartments. It was like having a frat house right next door to a sorority house. Sometimes Zeke and I would get in their way, as far as dating was concerned, and sometimes they would get in our way. However, we always remained good friends. The Ques and AKAs formed a very strong bond that school year. This was largely in part to the Smoketree Apartment Que-AKA connection. We threw several house parties and many of our *Sands* from other colleges would come in town and party with us. The spring '86 Lines at Virginia State (Nu Psi) and NCCU (Tau Psi) had established a strong bond with my LBs at A&T. But times were not all good at Smoketree. There was plenty of drama and a few domestic disturbances. Sometimes, our reputation of being womanizers would catch up with us. On one occasion, this caused a woman to throw rocks through my bedroom window when I wouldn't answer the door. I figured that it would be better to not answer the door and deal with a broken window than to open the door and watch a fight with the girl I had in my bedroom. I eventually called the police and filled out a police report. I told them I had no idea who did it, even though I know exactly who did it (and why). We eventually broke up after a few heated arguments and fights.

Sonja Comes into the Picture

I met Sonja while working at UPS. She was a clerk and I was an unloader. I would come in early and prep all the trucks for our work shift. She walked by with a clipboard in her hand, acting all shy and professional. We exchanged small talk and eventually I gave her my phone number. We talked on the phone for a few weeks before I asked her out on a date. Sonja invited me over for dinner a few times and I got to know her parents real well. My relationship with Sonja steadily blossomed and we soon started dating on a regular basis.

Lower Junior Year

During the the fall '88 semester, me and a few of my LBs met with the Dean of Student Affairs, our District Representative, and our chapter advisors. The purpose was to discuss the reinstatement of the Mu Psi Chapter. We had met all the university and fraternity requirements and they agreed we should be reinstated early. Mu Psi was back on the yard! This was great news. We immediately started making plans to conduct a spring line. So many guys had approached us about wanting to join our fraternity. I was the chapter president at the time and there were only four of my LBs still left in school. Everyone else had graduated and moved on with their lives. We kept them informed as to what was going on with the chapter. We held our interest meeting in January 1989 and over 100 guys showed up to express interest. Since we were just getting back on the yard, the local Greensboro graduate chapter (Tau Omega) assisted us with the entire process. We successfully pledged our first line since joining the fraternity. The spring '89 Line was a success and now we had about twenty Ques on the yard. There was purple and gold everywhere. We had members on the football team, the student government, the honor society, and many other programs.

My Military Commissioning, May '89

The Aggies' Battalion Commissioning Ceremony for spring '89 was the culminating event for me, having arrived at NC A&T as an Army PVT before becoming an ROTC Cadet. Now I was being bestowed with the honor of 2nd lieutenant. Earning the coveted *Gold Bar* signified the end of years of hard work and achievement. It meant a new beginning as a commissioned officer in the United States Army.

Granted by the president of the United States to a select group of individuals, officers are charged to defend their nation's liberty with honor and courage. It is a position of trust bestowed upon our nation's best and most dedicated young men and women. It was a very proud moment for me, my family and friends. I completed my Army ROTC requirements a year early because I had a five-year major. Even though I received my commissioning in 1989, I was not scheduled to go on active duty until the fall of 1990.

Senior Year

Finally, after years of juggling ROTC, Engineering classes, work, dating, and hanging out with the bruz, I was now a senior. What a journey. A lot of changes were taking place in the fall of 1989. I quit my job at UPS to concentrate on my Engineering studies. I was taking four difficult courses and I had to pass all of them in order to graduate in the spring. Sonja had pretty much been living with me for the last two semesters. I proposed to her that fall and she accepted.

We decided that she would move back home until we got married. She set the marriage date for May, 5 1990, which also happened to be my graduation weekend. Her parents approved of our plans and were happy that we were no longer shacking up.

Sonja and I had joined New Light Missionary Baptist Church a few years prior to getting engaged. Sonja's parents were members there too. We met with the Pastor, Dr. Cardes Brown, and received our pre-marital counseling. Sonja, her Mother and a few of the ladies at New Light Missionary Baptist Church proceeded with the wedding planning. They picked out the colors—teal green and peach—along with all the other details. In the meantime, I continued with my final semester of college. My courseload was heavy and there was no room for error. I had to pass all of my courses in order to graduate in May of 1990 and proceed onto active duty as planned. Everything was falling into place. As one of the senior Brothers on Campus, I had one final mission before departing. I had to train and assist our Neos during the planning, coordination and conduct of our spring 1990 line. The interested guys conducted their normal visits in order to express their interest in joining Omega Psi Phi. By February, we had selected the gentlemen who would eventually form the spring '90 Mu Psi Line. The pledge process went well. We only had a few minor issues which we were able to handle. We successfully pledged the spring 1990 Mu Psi Line. I felt good about leaving my beloved Chapter in the hands of our last two lines. My LBs and I prepared them well for the huge responsibilities they were undertaking.

Wedding / Graduation Weekend

The weekend of May 4-6, 1990 was one of the greatest weekends in my life. Not only did I get married to the love of my life, the former Sonja Fariecia Stallings, but I also graduated as a Distinguished Military Graduate (DMG) from North Carolina A&T with a Bachelor's of Science degree in Architectural Engineering. It was also one of the happiness and proudest weekends of my parents' life. I had put them through so much over the last six years and now it was finally paying off. The night of May 4 was the bachelor party. My Line Brothers, fraternity brothers and friends made sure I had a great time. We partied until about 3 a.m.

The Wedding, May 5, 1990

Saturday, May 5, 1990 was when Sonja and I got married. She was 23 and I was 24 at the time. Sonja and her Mom did an outstanding job of planning and coordinating everything for the wedding. For me (the groom), it was just a matter of surviving the bachelor party, and showing up at church on time. The groomsmen and I struggled to get up that morning. It was a rough night of partying but we survived it. We had breakfast and proceeded to the mall to pickup our tuxedos. Before we knew it, we were at the church and the wedding had started. The church was full with family, friends and fraternity brothers. Everything went just as planned. The wedding reception was held at the church fellowship hall. Following the reception, Sonja and I were driven to the hotel to start our honeymoon. Since my graduation was the next morning, we had to stay in town an extra night before heading to the mountains for our actual honeymoon getaway. We finally had a chance to relax and enjoy each other for a while.

May 6th, The Graduation

North Carolina A & T State University's Commencement program was a major event in Greensboro. The local residents and the University have a longstanding relationship over the the decades. Now it was my turn to walk across that stage and receive my Bachelor's in Architectural Engineering. It was a joyous occasion for me, my family and my friends. Everyone who knew me was aware of the struggles I endured over the past six years in order to get to graduation day. They were most proud of me for not giving up during the journey.

May 7th, the Honeymoon Getaway

After spending two extra nights in Greensboro. Sonja and I departed on Monday, May 7th for our honeymoon. We drove to the beautiful Blue Ridge Parkway along the eastern border of the legendary Shenandoah Valley. Outstanding scenery and recreational opportunities make the Blue Ridge Parkway one of the most popular units of the National Park System. *America's Favorite Drive* winds its way 469 miles through mountain meadows and past seemingly endless vistas. Split-rail fences, old farmsteads and historic structures complement spectacular views of distant mountains and neighboring valleys. Sonja and I enjoyed our honeymoon immensely. We walked along the scenic trails, played tennis and utilized the great accommodations at the resort.

The Summer of 1990

We chilled with both sets of in-laws during the summer of '90 before heading off to the Engineer Officer Basic Training (EOBC). I was not scheduled to report for active duty until August, which meant that Sonja and I had most of the summer to ourselves. We spent a few weeks in Portsmouth with my parents first. We spent a lot of time picking their brains about marriage. We were excited but anxious about leaving college life and entering the real world. We found time to cookout, visit relatives and spend a little time at the beach. We then proceeded back to Greensboro and spent the rest of the summer at Sonja's parents' house. She returned to her job at UPS for a few months and I worked at a shipping plant for the summer. We made enough to pay our bills, contribute to the utilities, and save for our next vehicle.

ACTIVE DUTY MILITARY

Military Duty in Germany

I knew my fun-loving college days couldn't last forever. But I had to admit that those six years were some of the best times of my life. But all good things must come to an end, and now it was time for me to put my education and military training to use. So, in August of 1990, just a few months after getting married and graduating from college, I received my orders for active duty military. Things in the military were a little tense during that time. Operation Desert Storm kicked off while I was enroute to EOBC. The Persian Gulf War – lasting from August 2, 1990 to February 28, 1991 and code-named Operation Desert Storm – was a war waged by a UN-authorized coalition force from 34 nations led by the United States in response to Iraq's invasion and annexation of Kuwait. While this was going on, I found myself attending EOBC, which was a 12-week military course designed to prepare brand new engineer 2nd lieutenants for their new career in the U.S. Army. I ended up graduating in the top 10% of my EOBC class and earning a slot to the Scout Platoon Leaders' Course (SPLC) at Fort Knox, Kentucky. This course combined with EOBC to prepare me well for my first military assignment. In March, 1991, I arrived in Dexheim, Germany and took charge of 2nd Platoon, Echo Company, 12th Engineer Battalion, 8th Infantry

Division. The vast majority of the division had already deployed to Iraq by the time I arrived in Germany.

Operation Desert Storm ended a lot sooner than anticipated and my unit became part of the Rear Detachment Section of 8th ID. Several of my engineer buddies arrived at their units in time to participate in the tail end of Operation Desert Storm. I was extremely disappointed that I wasn't able to join them in Iraq. They came back from war with all kinds of awards and exciting war stories. I never told them but I really envied and respected them for what they had accomplished. Nevertheless, duty in Germany had more than its share of challenges. I received three years of outstanding engineer training while serving in Germany. My unit, the 12th Engineer Battalion, was located about thirty miles from the historic Rhine River. At least once a month, we transported our ribbon bridge boats down to the Rhine and conducted bridging and rafting operations. It was part of our mission and it was also extremely adventurous. My soldiers and I looked forward to this monthly training event. Being stationed in Europe had its share of pros and cons. After my year as a Ribbon Bridge Platoon Leader, our entire unit relocated to Mannheim. We became part of the 3rd Brigade, 1st Armored Division. We trained hard and often. Our training cycle consisted of a 30-day *train-up* at our local training area (LTA), followed by 30 days at Gunnery (in Grafenheor) and 30 days at the Combat Maneuver Training Center (CMTC) in Hoenfels, Germany. We conducted this training cycle twice a year. So, as you can imagine, this meant a lot of time away out in the woods and away from home.

I learned so much during my three years in Germany. The highlight of my training in Germany was when my platoon won runner-up in the USAREUR-wide Sapper Stakes Engineer Competition in 1992. This grueling competition evaluated the top engineer squads and platoons in Germany as they competed against each other during a series of engineer training events, including an obstacle course, a physical fitness test, written assignments and numerous physically and mentally demanding combat engineer tasks. Our medals were presented to us by the Commanding General and Command Sergeant Major of USAREUR. My Battalion Commander, LTC Robert Cadow, was extremely proud of our accomplishments. I was just as proud of my fellow soldiers as well. Our months of dedicated training had finally paid off.

The Social Side of Germany

By no means were our three years in Germany all training related. When we were not in the field, there was plenty to see and do. Sonja and I took full advantage of the sightseeing tours, trips and local events. There were plenty of social activities to occupy our after-work time. Theta Rho International Chapter of Omega Psi Phi was one of the premier graduate Chapters in our beloved fraternity. I had the distinct pleasure of meeting and fellowshipping with Omega men from all over the U.S. The vast majority were military personnel assigned overseas. Each month we would conduct a formal meeting and fundraiser in a different town. By the time I had completed my three-year tour in Germany, I had visited every major city in the country. We were known for our lively parties, stepshows, train rides, and Mardi Gras. One of our unit's annual formal events was the Engineer Ball. This event was held every winter at our Officers' Club Ballroom. The spouses really enjoyed it because it gave them an opportunity to dress up in their formal gowns, eat, drink and socialize with other military couples in a very romantic, historical environment. My Masonic Lodge, the Wise Men Military Lodge # 125, sponsored several dances while we were stationed in Germany. We had the opportunity to raise a lot of money and contribute significantly to the local community.

Sonja and I initially lived in a small German town about ten minutes from our military post. Our neighbors were great. We participated in all local winefests, Oktoberfests, and other local holiday festivities. As our tour in Germany was coming to an end, we hated to leave the country, but we knew that our time was up. It was time to move on to our next assignment. Sonja took it kind of hard. She did not like the idea of leaving all the great friendships. For me, it was just part of military life.

Fort Bragg; Home of the Airborne!

Following our tour in Germany, Sonja and I headed back to Fort Leonard Wood so I could attend the Engineer Officer Advance Course starting in March of 1994. We were not too thrilled with Fort Leonard Wood because there was very little to do and we were not there long enough for Sonja to get a job. Upon the completion of the Engineer Officer Advance Course, I was assigned to 20th Engineer Brigade (Combat) (Airborne) at Fort Bragg as the Brigade Assistant Operations Officer. I was extremely proud to be joining an airborne engineer unit. I had always dreamed about being a paratrooper at Fort Bragg. My Dad told me all the war stories from when he was a paratrooper there at Fort Bragg in the early 1960s. Things were a lot different back then.

I arrived at Fort Bragg just in time to deploy to Haiti with the Brigade (and 18th Airborne Corps) in support of Operation Restore Democracy. Before I deployed, Sonja and I purchased our first house. It was a small two-story townhouse on the outskirts of Fayetteville, North Carolina. We were both very proud of our new home.

Operation Uphold Democracy was an intervention designed to remove the military regime installed by the 1991 Haitian *coup d'état* that overthrew the elected President Jean-Bertrand Aristide. The operation was effectively authorized by the United Nations Security Council Resolution 940. The operation began with the alert of United States and its allies for a forced entry into Haiti. U.S. Navy and Air Force elements staged to Puerto Rico and southern Florida to prepare to support the airborne invasion, spearheaded by elements of United States Special Operations Command and the U.S. 82nd Airborne Division. The operation was directed by Commander, Joint Task Force 120 (JTF-120), provided by Commander, Carrier Group Two. The military mission eventually changed from a combat operation to a peace-keeping and nation-building operation at that point, with the deployment of the U.S.-led multinational force in Haiti. I was assigned to the 20th Engineer Brigade Headquarters and we spent the majority of our time repairing roads, buildings and various other infrastructure facilities which had been damaged during the fighting. We set up our headquarters at Camp Castle, about twenty miles from Port-au-Prince, the capital of Haiti. Our other mission was to assist throughout the country in establishing order and providing humanitarian services.

Upon my return from Haiti, I was selected to move down to the 37th Engineer Battalion (Combat) (Airborne) where I served as the Battalion Adjutant while I awaited my turn for Company Commander. At Fort Bragg, one of the prerequisites for taking company command was the successful completion of Jumpmaster School. This was a very academically and physically demanding course. I prepared myself for weeks and passed the course the very first time. I was now set to take command in November, 1996. The change–of–command ceremony took place on Sicily Drop Zone. We conducted an airborne operation and landed on the drop zone approximately 100 meters from the ceremony area.

We then gathered up the entire company and marched over to the ceremony area. My parents, wife, fraternity brothers, friends and coworkers joined us for this very special occasion. Being a former Fort Bragg paratrooper himself, I could see the pride and excitement gleaming in my father's eyes. My mother was equally proud.

This was clearly one of the proudest days in my entire military career. I went on to commanded Charlie Company, 37th Engineer Battalion (Combat) (Airborne) from November 1996 until May 1998. Those were the best eighteen months of my military career. My engineer company completed numerous deployments, construction projects, training exercises and airborne operations. One of my most rewarding deployments was our trip to the Dominican Republic, where we completed multiple engineer construction projects, including building an elementary schoolhouse and upgrading and extending an airfield runway. While in the country, we were able to train extensively with our international partners. We ended this six-month deployment by conducting a combined airborne operation and earning our Dominican jump wings. The Dominican Republic had some of the most beautiful beaches and resorts. The people were very friendly and hospitable. They treated us very well. By the time we were scheduled to leave, several of my soldiers had fallen in love with local Dominican women and were considering marriage.

Once I returned from Dominican Republic, I was able to become active again with my fraternity. I joined the Tau Gamma Gamma chapter at Fort Bragg and immediately became active within the chapter. During my tour at Fort Bragg, I served as the Chapter Keeper of Peace, step team coordinator, and Dean of Stepping for our spring '95 line. Being stationed in North Carolina afforded me the chance to travel to Greensboro fairly often. Sonja and I were able to visit her parents and our college classmates on a monthly basis. The spring of 1995 was very special because I had the distinct privilege of being involved in the pledging of two lines, the spring '95 TGG Line at Fort Bragg and the spring '95 Mu Psi line at my alma mater. I also had a chance to attend many of the Fayetteville State University football games and meet many of the Brothers on their campus as well.

Sonja and I visited a few different churches in Fayetteville before finally joining Mount Olive Missionary Baptist Church. The congregation was very hospitable and the Pastor was my homeboy from Norfolk. At the end of my Fort

Bragg tour, I came down on orders for an assignment in Puerto Rico. Prior to this assignment, I had to complete the Army CAS3 course held at Fort Leavenworth, Kansas. This was a requirement for all Army Captains. There were several Army Captains at Fort Bragg who had to attend this same course. I rode to Kansas with my Frat Brother and friend Parker, which was a long boring ride. I met even more bruz while there at CAS3. I enjoyed hanging out in Kansas City and attended a few Chiefs and Royals games. After I completed CAS3, Sonja shipped our furniture and car and flew to Puerto Rico.

From Puerto Rico to Atlanta

Following my first tour at Fort Bragg, I was assigned to 2d-348th Combat Support Battalion at Fort Buchanan, Puerto Rico. Here I was the Senior Engineer Observer Control/Trainer. I was responsible for training, mentoring and evaluating over one thousand engineer officers, NCOs and soldiers throughout Puerto Rico. My job required me to travel to various engineer units on a monthly basis. It was a great experience in every way. I was able to see many beautiful scenes and tourist attractions and meet a lot of wonderful people. In addition to maintaining this challenging position, I enrolled in graduate school. It was very stressful but I was able to earn my MBA in Industrial Management while I was stationed in P.R. Sonja went to school and worked too.

Being stationed in Puerto Rico afforded Sonja and me the chance to take advantage of some great tourist opportunities. At least once a month, we would take a trip to some destination there on the island. We frequented the local beaches in sunny San Juan on a regular basis. One of our favorite tourist attractions was the legendary El Yunque Rain Forest. El Yunque is the local name for the Caribbean National Forest in Puerto Rico. El Yunque is the only tropical rain forest in the United States National Forest System. A rain forest is a quiet place but at El Yunque you can hear the occasional coquí or two chirping in the middle of the day. The ground is wet and muddy and is shaded by tall trees. The trees have huge trunks with small plants growing on them. There are vines hanging from their branches. There are small insects flying amid the rain, fog, or mist. On the trees you might see colorful birds, and butterflies. Many other animals hide in the branches and even under leaves on the ground. The abundant rainfall is shed through rocky rivers, creating many cascades of waterfalls and pools. Everywhere you look is green. Sonja and I were in the best shape of our lives. We were working out everyday, eating healthy and taking care of our mind, body and soul. We finished as runners-up in mini-triathlon (Sonja swam and I biked and ran).

Just like during our previous assignments, one of the first things Sonja and I did upon arriving at Fort Buchanan was find a place to worship. We eventually settled on the Post Chapel, where we actively participated in the gospel service. It was very rewarding spiritually and socially. We were able to meet and fellowship with some great Christian people. During the same time we were relocating to Puerto Rico, the U.S. Military was going through some major base realignments. The military bases in Panama were closing down and some of those units were reassigned to Puerto Rico. The Nu Gamma Gamma chapter of Omega Psi Phi was chartered and located at Fort Clayton, Panama. During this military realignment, NGG was transferred to Fort Buchanan, PR. I served as the Chapter *Vice Basileus* (Vice President) and assisted with the pledging process for the spring 2000 line.

One of the main hazards of being stationed in the Caribbean is the possibility of hurricanes. On September 19, a hurricane watch was issued for Puerto Rico. A day later on September 20, the watch was upgraded to a hurricane warning for the entire island. The warning was discontinued on September 22 at 1500 UTC. More than 1,600 people sought shelter in public buildings on Puerto Rico and the nearby U.S. Virgin Islands. Both areas declared a state of emergency and activated the United States National Guard for help. Puerto Rico's governor, Pedro Rosselló, began a ban on all liquor sales and forced the police to open all the shelters across the island. Banks and schools closed and flights were canceled as Puerto Rico braced for the upcoming impact. More than 1,000 people left their homes for shelters in the towns of San Juan, Arecibo and Mayaguez.

My engineer section was tasked to assist the local government with recovery efforts. We were attached to an U.S. Marine Taskforce for roughly four months. We assisted FEMA in support of the region's response and recovery operations in the aftermath of Hurricane Georges. Puerto Rico was hit very hard by this hurricane. The agricultural sector of Puerto Rico lost more than 50% of its crops and 65% of its poultry. Damages to houses were catastrophic, with 28,005 houses being completely destroyed. Another 72,000 were partially destroyed. On the nearby island of Culebra, 74 houses were completely destroyed with 89 getting partial damage. Schools suffered an estimated $20-25 million in damage. A total damage estimate on Puerto Rico totaled $1.907 billion. After months of recovery, things started to get back to normal. Sonja and I would eventually complete our assignment there and head off to our next assignment.

The ATL

In July 2000, I was assigned to 3rd Army/ARCENT at Fort McPherson, GA, where I was the C7 Construction Division Chief. I was stationed in Atlanta but our forward headquarters were in Kuwait. Things were moving along very well. The wife and I really enjoyed living in Atlanta. We worked during the week and became tourists on the weekend. We went to Falcons football games, Hawks basketball games, and the Dr. MLK Jr. Memorial. We also had family in the area. Alveta and her family lived about fifteen minutes away, while my brother-in-laws Wayne and Chris lived close by as well.

9/11

It was during this assignment that the 9/11 terrorist attacks happened. I remember that morning very vividly. I was in my office when I got the news. Our entire engineer section immediately ran down to the conference room and turned to the news channel. Like most people, I thought I was watching some sort of crazy movie as I saw the video clip of the planes crashing into the World Trade Center. I could not believe it. These horrible events forever changed the world. I was selected to immediately deploy to Kuwait IOT to help setup our forward headquarters. This was a very stressful time for all of us. Having just missed my opportunity to deploy to Desert Shield in 1991, I took great pride in being able to defend our country now.

In November 2001 I deployed to Kuwait and Afghanistan with the ARCENT Forward Headquarters in support of Operation Enduring Freedom. I spent a year in Kuwait/Afghanistan during my first Combat Tour (OEF1). God's grace and mercy protected me the entire time, through all the bombings, mortar attacks, IEDs, and attempted convoy ambushes. At the end of my first tour, I returned to Atlanta and prepared for my PCS back to Fort Bragg.

Fort Bragg (Part II)

I returned to Fort Bragg in 2004. I enjoyed Fort Bragg so much during my first assignment that I decided to return for a second tour. This is fairly common within the Airborne community. Most people either love Fort Bragg or hate the place. I was assigned to the 18th Airborne Corps Headquarters as the Deputy of Joint Exercises. I enjoyed this assignment because it gave me the opportunity to travel and experience even more exciting places throughout the world. From there, I was selected to do another six-month deployment to Kuwait and Iraq. I was billeted at Camp Arifjan, which just happened to be the same camp I helped design the previous year. I walked around Camp Arifjan with great pride knowing that I played a significant role in its design and construction.

But Camp Arifjan, just like all the other military camps, was not immune to enemy attacks. We frequently got bombed, attacked with mortars and shot at. I experienced several close calls with IEDs as we left camp to conduct our missions. It was a hectic and dangerous time, but we overcame our fear and completed our missions. Growing up in the 'hood had nothing on the war we were fighting in Iraq. The enemy hated the Americans and didn't mind losing their lives in order to take ours.

Upon my return from Iraq, I was selected to become the Brigade Operations Officer of the 20th Engineer Brigade (Combat) (Airborne). Having served in this unit as a captain prepared me well for this challenging assignment. I was in charge of overseeing that all day-to-day operations of the brigade and its subordinate units were conducted to standard. After serving as the Brigade Operations Officer, I moved up and became the Brigade Executive Officer. I was responsible for consulting with colleagues and superiors about all personnel decisions within the brigade. One of my first tasks when I took over was to prepare the brigade and subordinate units for another deployment to Iraq. This would be the second deployment in two years for most of the Officers, NCOs and soldiers. Nevertheless, morale remained high and most of us were ready and willing to deploy again.

Obviously, it was extremely tough on the families. Sonja and I had been struggling trying to keep our fragile marriage afloat. This deployment to Iraq was much different than my previous deployment. Conditions in the country had worsened and the tensions were very high during this time. We were based at Camp Victory in Baghdad. I was in charge of planning and coordinating all combat engineer tasks in the country. It was a very demanding job, but with God's grace and mercy, I was able to successfully complete this tour in Iraq and return home safely.

Being back at Fort Bragg also meant being able to rejoin the Tau Gamma Gamma Chapter of Omega Psi Phi, the "Airborne Ques". TGG had a very strong reputation within the fraternity and I also enjoyed being a part of this progressive chapter. I served as Vice Basileus and won the Superior Service award for my involvement in the local church and community.

PCS'd to Fort Carson

Upon my safe return from Iraq, I was selected to serve as the Battalion Executive Officer (XO) of a Field Artillery Battalion at Fort Carson, CO. This was a unique and prestigious opportunity I could not refuse. So I shipped my military supplies, loaded up my vehicle, and headed to Colorado Springs. I worked with some great Field Artillery Officers and NCOs. I taught them a lot about combat engineering while they taught me about Field Artillery. One of our most important missions was training the personnel who were about to deploy to Iraq and Afghanistan. I was able to use my previous deployment experience during this training. While living in Colorado Springs, I was able to attend Denver Broncos and Denver Nuggets games since Denver was only forty miles away from Colorado Springs. Of course, one of the first things I did after getting situated was locate my fraternity brothers. I had sent them an email before arriving in the area so they were expecting me. The Xi Pi Chapter was the name of the local chapter in Colorado Springs. It was made up of a combination of active duty, retired and civilian Brothers. Several of them I had met or heard about during previous assignments. I got involved of several of the Chapter's community service projects, including the Senior Mentorship Program, Mardi Gras, Step Team Coordinator, and mentorships at local schools. While I was stationed at Fort Carson, I had another close encounter with death. This one was not OIF/OEF related. I was involved in a car accident on the way back from a sporting event in Denver. I totaled my BMW X5 but walked away without a scratch. I learned it was true that God looks out for babies and fools. Drinking and driving was the cause of my accident. I had a little too much to drink and should not have been behind the wheel at that time. By the grace of God, I was not charged with a DUI. The Colorado State Trooper was a Military Veteran and gave me a break.

Dad's Illness and Passing

My father got sick while I was stationed at Fort Carson. I went home to visit him and help out around the house. He was going through chemotherapy for lung cancer and was starting to lose weight. I stayed for about three weeks before returning to Colorado. But my Dad's situation eventually got worse. He was diagnosed with terminal lung cancer. Alveta left Atlanta and moved back home. She and Michelle attended to my Dad. They called me one weekend; I still remember the phone call. It was a very emotional time in our family. I submitted paperwork requesting a compassionate reassignment to Virginia so I could help tend to my parents. My Mom was also recovering from a nervous breakdown at the time.

My paperwork was approved and within a few days, and I quickly packed up and headed back home. That fifteen-hour drive was the longest, most emotional trip in my entire life. So many thoughts were running through my head. I moved back into my parents' house when I got home. Alveta moved back into her old room and I moved back into mine. My Dad had added a garage and family room so there was a little more room now than when we were growing up. They say it takes a village to raise a child, but I learned it also take a village to care for an elderly person. My entire neighborhood pitched in and helped my sisters and I attend to my parents. It was one of the most heart-warming experiences of my entire life. I will be forever grateful to them.

I worked at TRADOC at Fort Monroe in Hampton during the day and helped care for my parents in the evenings. My Dad eventually lost his battle with cancer and died in 2007. Mom took the news in stride, having never fully recovered from her nervous breakdown. My Dad's home-going celebration was huge at New First Baptist Church Taylorsville (NFBCT). He had established a very strong reputation within the city, church, local community, and extended family. During my Dad's illness and the days prior to his death, I found out some interesting alarming developments about my Dad. It turned out I had a step-sister, named Barbara, and two step-brothers, named Leon and Alonzo, whom my Dad fathered when he was stationed at Fort Lawton, Oklahoma in the early 1960s. Barbara actually came to Virginia to see my Dad before he passed away. It was during that visit that she met Michelle, Alveta and me. For me, it was a very sensitive situation and I was initially reluctant to accept this. The most amazing part was the ages of each of us. Alveta is 53, Alonzo is 50, Barbara is 49, Leon is 48, I am 47 and Michelle is 44 years old. Wow! Pappa was a rolling stone.

My Dad passed away on May 13, 2007 at 3 am on Mother's Day. I remember the call I received from Alveta early that morning. There was very little she needed to say. The call was short, surreal and quiet. I immediately knew what had happened. It took my family awhile to get over my father's death. He was such a strong part of our family, community and church. It was tough on everyone. The part that allowed us to move on was the satisfaction of knowing that my father had accepted Christ and was in a better place. No more suffering, no more chemo, no more medicines. Alveta and Roland eventually moved back to Atlanta. I came up on orders for Korea and began my preparation for my next military assignment. Sonja returned to Greensboro and re-enrolled at NC A&T to finish her Bachelor's degree. Michelle and her family moved back in with our mother to help care for her. Those same neighbors helped out again, along with CNAs and volunteers. What a blessing they were.

It was a relief for me to know that Mom was being taken care of while I was serving my country in Korea. Michelle, CNAs and neighbors were able to handle things at home with Mom for awhile. But eventually she would end up having to be admitted into Sentara Nursing Home, which was about five minutes from her house. Michelle and her family would continue to visit her daily. I called weekly and spoke with Mom to let her know I missed her.

LIFE IN SOUTH KOREA

History Trivia

The history of South Korea formally begins with the establishment of South Korea on August 15, 1948. In the aftermath of the Japanese occupation of Korea, which ended with Japan's defeat in World War II in 1945, Korea was divided at the 38th parallel north in accordance with a United Nations arrangement, to be administered by the Soviet Union in the north and the United States in the south. The Soviets and Americans were unable to agree on the implementation of Joint Trusteeship over Korea. This led in 1948 to the establishment of two separate governments, each claiming to be the legitimate government of all of Korea. Eventually, following the Korean War, the two separate governments stabilized into the existing political entities of North and South Korea. The military demarcation line (MDL) of separation between the belligerent sides at the close of the Korean War forms North Korea's boundary with South Korea. A demilitarized zone (DMZ) extends for 2,000 meters (just over 1 mile) on either side of the MDL. Both the North and South Korean Governments hold that the MDL as only a temporary administrative line, not a permanent border. Initially established as Camp Jackson and still referred by that name sometimes, Camp Red Cloud is located in Uijeongbu, north of Seoul and relatively close to the DMZ. The military base was renamed in the memory of Mitchell Red Cloud Jr., an American hero awarded with the Medal of Honor. The base spreads over 164 acres. It supports a wide variety of units and types of military actions.

I was assigned to The 2nd Infantry Division at Camp Red Cloud. Our primary mission was the defense of South Korea in the event of an invasion from North Korea. I had the distinct honor of serving as the Division Engineer. I had heard a lot about Korea during my many years in the military but had never really considered being stationed there. Having already served two tours in Iraq and one in Afghanistan, my engineer branch assignment officer offered me South Korea. Sonja remained back in Greensboro to complete her college degree so I decided to accept the assignment. It turned out to be one of my better deployments. By being a forward deployment unit we were just a few miles from the infamous "DMZ". North Korean soldiers were on one side and South Korean soldiers were on the other side of the border. The two countries despised each other and made that perfectly clear. As an ally of the South Koreans, the U.S. played the role of peacemakers. However, everyone knew that if a conflict broke out, the Americans would definitely side with South Korea.

Life being stationed that close to the DMZ had its own share of challenges. The 1st Infantry Division stayed on alert for the vast majority of my time in South Korea. We had to be ready to respond at short notice to any situation that happened near the DMZ. In addition to being the Division Engineer, I was also the Division's Force Protection Officer. Throughout my time in South Korea, on any given weekend local residents – most radical college students – demonstrated in protest near the front gates of many of the U.S. military installations. My job was to create a response plan and ensure that each U.S. military installation was prepared to handle these scheduled demonstrations. Most of the demonstrations were non-violent but every once in a while, one of them would get out of hand, causing the local police to injure someone.

The weather in South Korea was characterized by four distinct seasons; spring began during the middle of April and was rather short in most parts of the country. Yellow sand dust originating in the Mongolian desert, occasionally invaded Korea during early spring and caused low visibility and eye irritation. This caused me some major problems with my allergies. The summer can be divided into two periods; *changma*, a rainy period that occurs during the early summer months and *hanyorum*, a hot and humid period falling in the late summer. The weather during the *changma* period was characterized by prolonged rainfall. More than 60 percent of the annual precipitation was concentrated between June and July. Much of the rainfall was due to summer monsoons that originate in the Pacific Ocean. Autumn was the season with crisp weather, plenty of sunlight and changing autumn leaves. This was the transitional season between the hot and humid summer, and the cold and dry winter months.

Traditionally, Koreans enjoyed the season of harvest *ch'usok* which was one of the most important national holidays in Korea. It was celebrated as a harvest festival, and occasionally referred to as the Korean version of the American Thanksgiving. The monsoonal arctic air from the interior of the Asian continent would bring bitter cold and dry weather along with occasional snowfall, adding warmth to the cold and dry winter weather periodically. Significant regional climate variations were caused by differences in elevation and proximity to the seas along with differences in latitude.

As I normally did with all my new assignments, I linked up with the bruz upon arriving in country. The Lambda Xi Chapter, which was another international chapter I had the distinct opportunity to associate with, had a long and proud history in South Korea. Lambda Xi Chapter was the first black Greek fraternity founded in the Republic of Korea. It was founded on February 22, 1977, at the Eighth United States Army (EUSA) headquarters, Yongsan, South Korea by 11 great Omega men. Over the past 35 years, the men of Lambda Xi have proudly served with distinction on the Korean Peninsula. We have fully embraced our responsibilities in the Korean/US community. Whether assisting the less fortunate or uplifting those striving for academic excellence, the wide range of talents and expertise amongst the brotherhood enabled us to routinely take on tasks that most would deem too difficult to accomplish.

Two of the key fundraising events I participated in were the the Legendary Que Boatride and the Mardi Gras. People flew in from all over the Pacific Coast to attend these events. We took great pride in putting together a top-notch event. Due to the fact that I resided at Camp Red Cloud up near the DMZ, I was not authorized to have a vehicle. Whenever I had a free weekend, I would take the shuttle bus up to Area II in Seoul and hang out with the bruz. Two buildings I spent a lot of time in at Camp Red Cloud were the Chapel and the gym. Our Sunday worship service was well-organized and very powerful. Officers and soldiers alike looked forward to attending these weekly services. Serving in South Korea was tough duty and the CRC Chapel family was our outlet. CRC Chapel was a place where I could decompress after a stressful week at work. The Camp Red Cloud gym opened early and closed late, which gave me the opportunity to work out everyday (and sometimes twice a day). There were very few other distractions, which allowed me to focus on improving my health spiritually, physically, and emotionally.

Halfway through my tour in South Korea, I returned home to Virginia for Christmas break and spent four weeks with my family. I visited my Mom daily at Sentara Nursing Home. We talked and prayed together often. She was still mourning the death of my Dad and it was beginning to affect her health. In addition to depression, she was also dealing with dementia and Alzheimer's disease. Soon after I completed my one-year assignment in Korea and was able to pull some strings and get stationed near home again. I accepted an instructor's position at the Joint Forces Staff College (JFSC) in Norfolk, about fifteen minutes from home. I spent a month with Mom before starting my new assignment. Even with dementia and Alzheimer's disease setting in, my mother was still able to counsel me and give me some sound marital advice. She loved Sonja dearly and did not want Sonja to go through some of the same problems that she went through with my Dad. I would come over to the nursing home twice a day to visit Mom and have a heart-to-heart talk. It was usually a one-way conversation. I sat there and listened as Mom discussed a lot of things that she had been holding inside for years. This poem *Mother to Son* reminds me of the last conversation that Mom and I had before she passed away. I made a promise to her that I would live the remainder of my life in such a way that would allow me to reunite with her and my Dad in Heaven.

MOTHER TO SON
by Langston Hughes

Well, son, I'll tell you:
Life for me ain't been no crystal stair.
It's had tacks in it,
And splinters,
And boards torn up,
And places with no carpet on the floor—
Bare.
But all the time
I'se been a-climbin' on,
And reachin' landin's,
And turnin' corners,
And sometimes goin' in the dark
Where there ain't been no light.
So, boy, don't you turn back.
Don't you set down on the steps.
'Cause you finds it's kinder hard.
Don't you fall now—
For I'se still goin', honey,
I'se still climbin',
And life for me ain't been no crystal stair.

Mom passed away in August, 2009 at Sentara Nursing Home, about six blocks from her home in the Cavalier Manor section of Portsmouth. Michelle met me at the nursing home and we cried for awhile as we sat down and stared lovingly at our mother. The amazing thing was that she looked so at peace. All the suffering, pain, medication and relapses were now gone. She was in a better place. We called Alveta and gave her the news. Alveta and Roland arrived the next day and we immediately started planning our mother's "Homegoing Celebration". She was known and loved by so many people. We were concerned about being able to fit everyone in our church. But, of course, God made it all work. It was a very emotional yet jubilant funeral. Everyone knew about the pains and struggles Mom had endured over the years. But they also knew that God had a much bigger plan for her.

The Aftermath of Mom's Death

I was a momma's boy all the way—tough on the outside but sensitive, kind and emotional on the inside. Life at home without Mom and Dad was extremely difficult for the entire family. My parents had been fixtures in the Cavalier Manor Community for over forty years. It was strange not having them around. Throughout my life, my parents had been my #1 cheerleaders, supporters, and motivators. They were truly the wind beneath my wings. What got me through these difficult times was my faith in God and knowledge that they were in a better place now, reunited in Heaven. I also knew that, in order for me to see them again, I had to get my personal life in order so that I too could make it to Heaven. This was the motivation I needed, allowing me to refocus my entire life. I now live my life not just for me, but also for the fact that I cannot let my parents down. This is what gives me that renewed joy and strength as I move on with my life.

The Rekindling of my Marriage

But from the beginning of creation, 'God made them male and female.' 'Therefore a man shall leave his father and mother and hold fast to his wife, and the two shall become one flesh.' So they are no longer two but one flesh. What therefore God has joined together, let not man separate." Mark 10:6-9

Even though my military career was going very well, my marriage was suffering for several reasons. My infidelity in 1999 resulted in my 14-year-old son, Brandon. Though Sonja eventually forgave me, our marriage has never been quite the same. It took the grace and mercy of God himself to prevent my wife from leaving me at that time. Add to that the fact that I was obsessed with having a successful military career. I was sacrificing family time in order to ensure job success. The fraternity was taking up way too much of my time too. The volunteering, mentoring and community service were all good things. But sometimes, too much of a good thing can be detrimental. And then there was the hanging out, partying, and drinking. Sonja and I knew that we would have to do something soon in order to save our dying marriage. Getting back to being active in the church was definitely a step in the right direction. But I knew that I had to do one of those man in the mirror self-assessments. I had to change and I had to do it immediately. *The Man in The Mirror* is a famous song sung by the late Michael Jackson. It applied perfectly to my life. Being a better person is the essence of fixing nearly any troubled romance. Therefore, I knew that I had the best chance of rekindling my marriage was through rebuilding our communication and trust, and by becoming a better person. Seldom is there a time when it can harm you to make improvements in your life.

With that in mind, I found find this to be a very opportune time to take stock of my communication skills, mannerisms, and romantic behavior patterns. Once we got moved in and set up in our new house, we needed to find a good church to attend. My home church, NFBCT, was about 25 minutes away from where we lived. We wanted to find something closer to home. We visited two churches before a neighbor recommended Mount Lebanon Missionary Baptist Church (affectionately known as *The Mount*). Sonja and I immediately fell in love with it. The people were very friendly, the Pastor (Bishop Kim Brown) was a great preacher, and the choir was one of the best that we had ever heard. Bishop Kim Brown and Elder Valerie K. Brown made a great ministry team. Bishop Brown was also from Portsmouth and knew several of my family members and friends.

On "Watch Night," December 31, 2009, Sonja and I decided to join "The Mount" and become partners of this great fellowship. Growing up in church, I had always been active wherever I was stationed. I decided to join the Men's Usher Board (known as the Doorkeepers) and Sonja joined the Greeters. It was a pleasure to be able to assist worshipers before and during church service. It took this assignment very seriously. Later, with the leadership of Bishop Brown, a Men's Fellowship (called Iron sharpens Iron) was organized. We met on Monday evening for one hour. It was a great opportunity for Christian men to meet and discuss pertinent items affecting all of us. My wife and I always made sure that we made time in our schedules to attend Wednesday evening Bible Study. Bishop Brown was not only a great minister but also was a great teacher. His ability to break the scripture down and present it in a way that the entire congregation could understand was amazing. One of the highlights during our three years at *The Mount* was *Issachar*.

Brandon's summer visits

My son Brandon is now fourteen. He resides in Jacksonville, Florida with his mother. Each summer for the past three years, I have flown him to Chesapeake, Virginia to spend part of the summer with Sonja and me. The first summer did not go well, mostly because he and I are both set in our ways. I attempted unsuccessfully to force the father-knows-best technique. Brandon, being a little bit spoiled and somewhat of a momma's boy himself, resented me for that. But the following two summers went much better. I guess I was getting soft as I aged. Brandon and I were able to form a strong father-son relationship. We both enjoyed many of the same activities like sports, hanging out at the beach, and spending time with family and friends. Sonja and Brandon have actually started to bond over the years as well. Sonja loves kids but has a no-nonsense approach when it comes to dealing with them. All in all, this situation has worked out much better than any of us could have anticipated.

Omega Psi Phi Fraternity, Inc.

During my time with the Zeta Iota Chapter, I served as the Social Action Committee Chairman. One of my key projects was the afterschool mentoring/ tutoring project (called *Project Uplift*) at Hodges Manor Elementary School. This was a joint collaboration between Zeta Iota Chapter, Portsmouth Public Schools, and the Boys & Girls Clubs of Southeastern Virginia. Our focus was helping students develop academically and personally. The Chapter Social Action Committee also conducted several other activities throughout the year such as;

- Adopt-A-Highway
- Thanksgiving Food Drive
- Christmas Toy Drive
- Christmas Can Food Drive
- Christmas Clothing Drive
- Portsmouth Food bank Donations

I was honored and humbled to have twice won the Superior Service Award (2009-2011) during my time with the Zeta Iota Chapter. This was a great and proud honor for me. To be able to come back to my hometown and participate in the Chapter that has produced so many strong leaders was a great feeling. Being able to mentor kids at the same schools I once attended was also a great honor and privilege as well. The P-town Que Reunion was one of the social events I always looked forward to. Portsmouth has a long and proud legacy of producing strong Omega Men, both in the local hometown Graduate Chapter (Zeta Iota) and at the numerous other Chapters throughout the U.S. The P-town Que Reunion was a chance for P-town Ques all over the world to come home, fellowship, celebrate and reflect on not only our great fraternity but our hometown lineage. Events included golf, barbecues, stepshows, and house parties. We normally concluded the event with a church service on Sunday morning, for those not too tired to attend. The highlight of the summer of 2010 was our National Convention. The 76th Conclave of the Omega Psi Phi was held July 22-30, 2010 in Raleigh. This event marked the Centennial Celebration (100 years) of our Fraternity. Omega Men from all over the World converged on The Convention Center in downtown Raleigh for this event. It was a very momentous occasion. The *Roadtrip* to the Centennial Celebration was a festive event within itself. Fraternity members traveled to D.C. by various modes of transportation (i.e., bus, train, carpool, or plane). I took the Amtrak from Newport News, Virginia to Washington, D.C. I met several fraternity Brothers on the train as we talked and fellowshipped for the entire train ride. In addition to celebrating the Centennial, my Chapter Line (Spring '86, Bloody Mu Psi) celebrated our 25th anniversary. My Line Brothers and I met in Raleigh and hung out for about four days. We attended meetings and seminars in addition to numerous parties and social events.

Family Matters

The family has always been a very important part of my life. Both of my parents have very close families. We call, email and text each other on a regular basis. Family reunions have always been special to me and my family. On my Dad's side, we celebrate the Sharpe-Bynum family reunion every summer. The reunion is normally rotated between Wilson, North Carolina and Hampton Roads, where several of my Dad's relatives moved to after leaving Wilson. The Wilson Memorial Chapel was one of the focal points for the Sharpe family. Several of my Dad's siblings attended that church and were eulogized there. The fellowship hall is normally where we hold these events. It was used by The Sharpe-Bynum family for numerous family reunions and special dinners. We have some of the best home cooking at these events, including Carolina BBQ, greens, baked beans, and numerous cakes and pies. And who could forget the "Soul Train" line, dance contest, health fairs and photo albums? As a kid, we learned a lot of family history (both the good and the bad), and many family secrets were found out during these reunions. I also got a chance to see folks whom I hadn't seen in years.

My Mom's maiden name is Person and she has a large but close family. The Person family reunions are celebrated during Homecoming back in my mom's hometown of Branchville, Virginia. It's held every first Sunday in August at Rising Star Baptist Church. Family members could come from all over the country, including New Jersey, New York, the Midwest, Texas, Ohio, Maryland, Georgia, and Florida. Immediately after the church service, there would be a big feast with all types of homemade country cooking. After spending a few days in the country, most of us would head for Virginia Beach for a week of swimming, biking, fishing, barbecuing and just relaxing on the beach. It is definitely one of our annual highlights.

Joint Forces Staff College (JFSC)

Teaching at the Joint Forces Staff College gave me the opportunity to work with some of the most talented and brightest officers and civilians from all over the world. The mission of the Joint Forces Staff College is to educate national security professionals to plan and execute operational-level joint, multinational, and interagency operations. It is also to instill a primary commitment to joint, multinational, and interagency teamwork, attitudes, and perspectives. This was a joint environment, which meant we had students from all branches of service, and from just about every one of our allies.

I was an instructor within the the Joint and Combined Warfighting School (JCWS). My job was to produce graduates capable of creatively and effectively planning operational level warfighting for joint and combined military forces, all while integrating the effects of the United States Government, non-governmental organizations, and international organizations to ensure the success of Combatant and Joint Task Force Commanders. The students learned a lot from the instructors but I have to admit that the instructors also learned some things from the students. The setting was in a college campus environment with classrooms, auditoriums, a gym, a library, stores and on-campus apartments. It was very hard to get assigned to JFSC. I also taught the Irregular Warfare Elective

Program, which allowed students to conduct in-depth studies of irregular warfare issues, which they found particularly useful.

It was a very competitive environment for the instructors and students alike. My seminar won several academic and athletic awards. The greatest part was the fact that I was back home, fifteen minutes from where I grew up. This allowed me to visit relatives and old friends whom I had not seen in several years. It also allowed me to give back to my hometown through volunteering and community service. This gave me a tremendous sense of pride and accomplishment.

Military Retirement

After 22 years of devoted service to the U. S. Army Corps of Engineers, it was time for a change. It was time to go in a different direction. The ironic thing was that I had never planned to make the military a career. I joined the Army ROTC while I was a student in college. I needed a way to pay for my out-of-state college expenses. ROTC was also a great way to stay in shape and learn some leadership skills. I eventually earned an Army ROTC Scholarship and went to Advance Camp. It was at Advance Camp at Fort Bragg that I started to excel in ROTC and was assessed for active duty. As a three-year ROTC scholarship recipient, I was obligated to serve six years on active duty. After my first six years, I was enjoying military life so much that I decided to stay in. Before I knew it, I had successfully completed ten years of service and was halfway to full retirement. It made no sense for me to get out of the military at that point, so Sonja and I decided to stick it out and do twenty years.

We arrived in Norfolk in August of 2009 for my final assignment. I could have submitted my retirement paperwork immediately upon arriving at my last assignment. However, I made a promise to myself that if my engineer assignment officer was able to get me back home for my last assignment, I would complete the entire three-year tour. I had mixed emotions as I approached military retirement. I really felt that I had plenty of fuel left in the tank and was looking forward to promotion to O-6 and at least one more deployment/assignment. But that was not in the cards. Selection rate for my year group was less than 35%. I was in the middle of the pack and had a 50/50 chance of getting selected for O-6. I had the option of staying in the military and going before the board again next year. However, there were so many other things I wanted to do with my life that I decided that this was the perfect time to make that transition out of the military.

Sonja and I had purchased our retirement home in Chesapeake, Virginia. Sonja was in graduate school at Norfolk State University and I had several job options I could pursue. We prayed on this subject for several weeks and then decided to submit our retirement paperwork in December, 2011, with an official retirement date of September 1, 2012. Because I was assigned to the Joint Forces Staff College at the Norfolk Naval Station, I was authorized to attend the Navy Executive-Transition Assistance Program (E-Tap). This is a one-week retirement/transition program for military officers in the rank of O-5 and above. The Navy E-Tap program was well-organized and allowed me to get a jump on my retirement/transition preparation. I prepared a draft resume and had it critiqued by the Navy E-Tap personnel. I was able to attend this program one year prior to my official retirement date. As I got closer to retirement, I was able to attend the Army Career and Alumni Program (ACAP) program at Fort Eustis in Newport News, Virginia. Established in 1990, the Army Career and Alumni Program (ACAP) is an integral part of the Army personnel lifecycle. ACAP provides comprehensive transition services to separating and retiring soldiers, Department of Army Civilians and their family members. ACAP Counselors deliver congressionally mandated pre-separation counseling, provide job search training, assist in the use of automated employment tools, conduct one-on-one counseling, and facilitate employment workshops/seminars. All soldiers deserve the best possible start in the civilian world when the time comes to leave the Army, and ACAP provides the knowledge and skills to smooth the way. There is no better recruiting influence in the community than a retiree or veteran whose Army experience includes being treated with respect and being supported even after making a decision to transition to civilian life. I was extremely satisfied with the services, counseling and advice I received through Army ACAP. I am forever grateful for all they did for me and Sonja during my transition.

My ACAP Counselors assisted me in creating more professional customized resumes for specific jobs and job fields. They also provided instruction as to how to use the Internet for transition and career research and to apply for civilian and federal jobs. The knowledge and skills ACAP provided me were instrumental in my smooth transition to the civilian workforce. The closer I got to my official retirement date (1 September 2012), the more anxious I got.

After 22 years of active duty military service, I was about to make a major career change. It was the unexpected that bothered me most. I spoke with numerous officers and NCOs who had already retired from the military, and they gave me some outstanding advice. I considered myself to be well-prepared and ready for this next challenge. Finally, the big day arrived. After days of meticulous planning and rehearsals, it was time for my retirement ceremony. The event was held at the Jacobs Theater at Fort Eustis, Virginia on June 15, 2012. Relatives from both sides of my family were in attendance to include Sonja, my in-laws, sisters, brothers-in-law, nieces and nephews, aunts, cousins, fraternity brothers, friends, and coworkers. My Mom and Dad were looking down from Heaven and I can only assume that they were proud of me. It was a very special and emotional day.

After the ceremony, we attended my retirement luncheon, which was held at the at Lakeside Restaurant at Fort Eustis. My retirement party was held that night at the American Legion Post in Portsmouth. It meant a lot to me to be able to conduct my retirement party in my hometown. It was the same American Legion that my Dad was a member of when he was living. In the U.S. Army, it is customary that the Retiree be *roasted* prior to retiring. *Roasting* was nothing more than an opportunity for family, friends and coworkers to pay tribute— whether good, bad, or indifferent—to the retiree. Each person had an opportunity to say something about me. Some comments were amusing while others were quite touching. Some comments were very true while others were only partly true. It was all meant to be in fun. The mayor of Portsmouth, Ken Wright, who happens to be a friend and fraternity brother of mine, was in attendance and gave some rousing comments on behalf of the City of Portsmouth. It made me feel good to end my military career in my hometown—the same town that played such a significant role in raising me from a young wanna-be thug into an Engineer Officer in the U.S. Army Corps of Engineer.

Transition Leave (1 July - 1 September 2012)

Two weeks after my retirement ceremony, I completed my final out-processing and signed out my unit on terminal leave. This simply gives an Officer, NCO or soldier the opportunity to take any unused leave prior to the official retirement date. In my case, I had sixty days of leave saved up, which meant I was able to stop work sixty days before my official retirement date. Therefore, I started my terminal leave on July 1, 2012. It was well-deserved and very needed. I finally had the opportunity to do some traveling, visit relatives I had not seen in awhile, relax at Virginia Beach, golf, fish and just chill for awhile. On September 1, 2012, I put on my military uniform for the last time, drove over to Fort Eustis, Va. and picked up my official retirement orders. This was truly a storybook ending to my military career. I could not have orchestrated it better myself.

Part VI
Lessons Learned along the Way

L earning lessons is a process that derives knowledge from experience to be applied to current and future projects. This is essential for avoiding the repetition of past failures and mishaps. The ultimate goal is to turn perceived deficiencies and recognizable best practices into lessons learned in order to improve effectiveness. Lessons learned systems are motivated by the need to preserve knowledge and convert individual experience into general knowledge, so that those who encounter a similar context or condition can benefit.

I retired from the United States Army on September 1, 2012. I spent 22 years bouncing around the globe for Uncle Sam and was ready to do something different with my life. I visited at least a dozen countries and experienced many cultures, but in my entire career had spent half that time in the United States. I spent several Christmases and Thanksgivings away from home. My family would mostly get to see me as I transitioned from one overseas base to another, where I would catch up on what happened in their world since the last time I was home. If I was lucky, I would be home during a birthday, a wedding or even a funeral. I really missed seeing my wife and watching my son, nieces and nephews grow up. I am looking forward to being a family man again. Listed below are the lessons that I learned during my journey.

ISSUE # 1: MAKING THAT TRANSITION FROM ROTC CADET TO COMMISSIONED OFFICER CAN BECOME VERY CHALLENGING AND STRESSFUL.

Discussion/Recommendation: Don't try to be a badass: Some people get their rank (butter bar) and decide that they rule the world. They walk around trying to be a hard-ass. Most of the time, people assume you're just trying too hard.

Don't compare cadet training to the real Army: Cadet training might have been great for your confidence and leadership, but comparing Army experience with Cadet experience may end up highlighting your inexperience as opposed to helping you relate to your soldiers. In general, it's best to stay away from such stories.

Don't assume you know it all: A brand new officer always has room to learn and grow. Be open to mentorship and advice. Be open about the fact that you are there to learn, adjust and do the best job that you can. Have a good attitude and don't be condescending. No one likes being talked down to by the new guy, no matter how much higher in rank they might be.

If you're Prior Service, don't try to be one of the guys: Using your experience as an enlisted soldier should feed your leadership style. But the line between you and your soldiers should always be clear. Don't try to be buddies. It's 100% okay to be friendly, but there should always be that respectful distance. The last thing you want is to look like you're playing favorites.

ISSUE # 2: LEADERS ENABLE PEOPLE

Discussion: Soldiers are always watching, and it is your job never to walk by a soldier without a greeting or word of encouragement. Encouragement is a combat multiplier.

Recommendation: Carry yourself in a way that encourages your soldiers to respect not only your rank but you as a person.

ISSUE # 3: MAKE YOUR OWN COFFEE

Discussion: Rank has its privileges. However, having my own office, parking spot, military vehicle with my name on the windshield, and a soldier to drive me places weren't the privileges of command. The privilege is the opportunity to serve soldiers in a larger capacity and to have a greater positive impact. I took the approach that I was there to serve the soldiers, and it helped me to establish the correct perspective and keep my ego in check. An absence of ego allows you to be humble. It allows you to laugh at yourself and to show your personality. When soldiers see you in this human light, dealing with the same basic aspects of living as they do, it removes you from the pedestal, whether you intend to be on one or not.

Recommendation: When you can, load your own kit, make your own photocopies, or make a pot of coffee at the office. Doing the seemingly menial tasks reveals you as a humble servant, while still being the commander. Our legacy rests in leading soldiers through tough missions while caring for their families. Soldiers need leaders' interest and concern.

ISSUE # 4: TAKE TIME TO SHARPEN YOUR AXE

Discussion: Oftentimes during my early career, I found myself always on the go. I was racing from one task to the next to the next—never taking a break, always trying to be the best officer in my unit. I was very competitive and did not want to give my peers a chance to catch me. What I learned over time is that I needed to take breaks to sharpen my axe. That was when I learned the lesson of taking time to reflect, think, pause, or just relax. I would take about fifteen minutes in the morning and evening, close my office door and just meditate. In addition, I would often use my lunch break to go to the gym. Working out and sitting in the sauna also helped me sharpen my axe. It helped me decompress, reflect, think, and relax. If we don't sharpen the axe often, it begin to dull. We will miss the big picture—or something critically important.

Recommendation: Take time to sharpen your axe and teach your subordinates to do the same.

ISSUE # 5: IT IS NOT JUST ABOUT REACHING YOUR DESTINATION

Discussion: The journey through life is just as important as reaching our final destination.

There is so much to be learned from our journey through life. Many times we rush through life trying to reach our goals/destinations as fast as we can.

Recommendation: Slow down, relax and enjoy the ride. Take time to enjoy the little things in life.

ISSUE # 6: GIVE BACK!

Discussion: I truly believe that in order to be truly and completely successful, you must give back to those in need. A generous and compassionate spirit is priceless. I have been amazingly blessed by just being a blessing to others. Giving back can be in the form of money, time, or advice.

Recommendation: As you climb up the ladder of success, always remember to give back along the way.

ISSUE # 7: LEARN FROM YOUR FAILURES IN LIFE

Discussion: We often tend to focus on our successes in life and overlook the great opportunity that we have to learn from our failures. Our ability to learn from failures will only make us stronger in our journeys through life.

Recommendation: Learn from your failures but do not dwell on them.

ISSUE # 8: UNDERSTAND PROSPERITY

Discussion: Prosperity is built upon progress, and progress is measured from the point at which we started. We do not compete on an equal playing field.

Recommendation: Acknowledge it and prepare for life accordingly. That preparation starts in elementary school.

ISSUE # 9: MONEY, THE ROOT OF ALL EVIL

Discussion: Many people allow money to become their sole driving force in life. What were you put on this earth to do? What is your purpose? Once you identify your purpose, it's just a matter of developing and implementing your plan.

Recommendation: Do not allow money to be your only driving force in life. You must have a purpose in life. Establish goals and objectives which will assist you in reaching those goals.

ISSUE # 10: ALWAYS MAKE IT A PRIORITY TO MAINTAIN A STRONG OFFICER-TO-NCO RELATIONSHIP WITHIN YOUR UNIT

Discussion: Most officers and NCOs get along great and work well together. But in some rare cases, the relationship is dysfunctional or could use some major improvements. During my entire military career, I made it a priority to establish and maintain a strong officer-to-NCO relationship. It definitely was a combat multiplier, both in garrison and in the field during deployments.

Recommendation: To establish and maintain a strong officer-to-NCO relationship. I recommend the following actions;

1. Conduct Your Counseling
2. Know Your Role and Stay in Your Lane
3. Be Good at Your Job
4. Treat Each Other with Mutual Respect
5. Always Keep the "Mission" as the Top Priority
6. Maintain Open and Honest Communication
7. Be Supportive and Loyal to Each Other

ISSUE # 11: YOU MUST LEARN TO LEAD FROM EVERYWHERE

Discussion: When responding to a complex, fast-moving crisis, leaders must constantly adapt their plans and remain flexible at all times. In a "multi-dimensional" asymmetric battlefield, leading from the front is no longer the most effective approach. Oftentimes, there is no clearly defined *front* or *rear*. The adversary's approach changes fast and is very unpredictable.

Recommendation: Learn to practice *Adaptive Leadership*

ISSUE # 12: POWERING DOWN LEADERSHIP IS ESSENTIAL IN TODAY'S ARMY

Discussion: According to long-held U.S. Army tradition, leadership is based on a rigid hierarchy. However, in today's modern warfare, particularly in Afghanistan, teams of soldiers are distributed across—and embedded in — an entire population. This has sparked a movement toward leadership training that covers not only the skills of single individuals, but the effectiveness of the teams they lead.

Recommendation: Learn to practice a Powering Down leadership style early in your military career.

ISSUE # 13: HOW TO DRESS AS A MILITARY OFFICER WHEN NOT IN MILITARY UNIFORM

Discussion: From my observations while coming up through the ranks, I noticed that the emphasis was always on how, when and where to wear your military uniform. Very little emphasis was placed on how military officers should dress when not wearing their official military uniform. For example, business casual is a phrase that is used quite liberally these days. Basically, the rule to remember is that business casual does not mean casual. It does not mean that you can dress however you want. It does not mean jeans and a T-shirt. You are still expected to look professional. For men, a business casual wardrobe should consist of several long-sleeved cotton Oxford shirts, a few cotton polo or golf shirts, chinos in acceptable colors (khaki, dark blue, olive green, or stone), wool slacks, and a sports coat.

Recommendation: Be cognizant of your appearance at all times and remember that you are representing the U.S. military whether you are on duty or off.

ISSUE # 14: TAKE TIME TO ENJOY YOUR FAMILY

Discussion: During my 22 years on active duty, I have witnessed too many friends and coworkers who enjoyed success in the military at the expense of losing their families. High tempers and intense work environments can make it extremely challenging to maintain a balanced family life. You really must make it a priority in order for it to work.

Recommendation: Make family time a priority early in your career and maintain that balance throughout your career.

ISSUE # 15: VOLUNTEER

Discussion: Volunteering is generally considered an altruistic activity, and is intended to promote good or improve human quality of life, which in return produces a feeling of self-worth and respect. Volunteering is also famous for skill development, socialization and fun. It is a great way for military spouses to make contacts for possible employment. Sonja and I made it a point to volunteer at each of our duty stations.

Recommendation: Get involved in your local community.

ISSUE # 16: SAVING FOR RETIREMENT

Discussion: After 22 years, I had acquired a home, truck, car, and furniture, but I had less than $20,000 in the bank. The rest was spent on some great times and adventures. Even though I receive retirement pay, I still live paycheck to paycheck. Several investment companies approached me when I was a young captain. However, I figured that since I was so young at the time, I would have plenty of time to start saving for retirement. Year after year, I continued to procrastinate and make excuses as to why I did not need to invest and save for retirement. Before I knew it, I was submitting my retirement paperwork and really did not have a retirement plan (other than going back to work).

Recommendation: Ensure that you have a plan and start saving early for retirement. It is never too early to start saving for retirement.

ISSUE # 17: MAKING THE TRANSITION FROM MILITARY TO CIVILIAN LIFE CAN BE DIFFICULT IF NOT PLANNED PROPERLY

Discussion: I know friends who made sudden decisions to leave the military and most of them are currently struggling to make ends meet. Finding a job after the military is very important, but it is not the only major adjustment. My living expenses have been considerably more in the civilian world. I experienced increases in housing, medical, dental and life insurance costs.

Recommendation: Ensure that you have a marketable skill or education. Carefully plan your post military life at least two years in advance. It is important to factor in all of the direct and indirect benefits you receive in the military and plan for them when you get out.

ISSUE # 18: HEALTHCARE

Discussion: In the military, if you weren't feeling well, you went to sick call. Mostly they gave you some drugs or ibuprofen and sent you on your way. It was considered somewhat macho to live with pain. As a young officer, I would rarely go to sick call. It was more of a pride and ego thing for officers at that time. However, I always knew that if it got too rough, I could go get free medical care. Of course, this also meant that you could physically exert yourself without a thought for the future. In the civilian world, you have HMOs and if you are extremely lucky they don't cost too much of your paycheck. Also, all of those physical injuries could be considered pre-existing and that would drive up the costs too. Lastly, your family was covered for free in the military, but that too drives up the price of healthcare.

Recommendation: Plan and prepare for your family's post-military healthcare needs while you are still on active duty.

In summary, live life to the fullest! Think about this: you are at the apex of human development. You are living in an age when change has become exponential rather than incremental. You have won the birth lottery by being born in the West in the late 20th century. Do not waste this opportunity. Have fun, play hard and work hard. But most importantly, be aware that you are in a position that 6 billion people around the globe would die to be in. Seize the moment!

Part VII
How to Become an Officer in the U.S. Army

Y ou may become an officer in the U.S. Army through one of four commissioning programs: the United States Military Academy, the Army Reserve Officers Training Corps (ROTC), the Officer Candidate School (OCS), or direct appointment. All require that the applicant be a high school graduate, pass a medical and physical exam, and be at least seventeen years old. To be competitive for these programs, an individual needs to be working toward or already have acquired a four-year college degree.

U.S. Military Academy

The United States Military Academy, located at West Point, New York, offers Bachelor of Science degree with majors in both Engineering and Liberal Arts. Graduates earn a commission as a Second Lieutenant in the U.S. Army. Admission to the academy is very competitive. Appointments are generally made through nominations from U.S. senators and representatives. Applicants should begin their quest for entry into the academy no later than the middle of their junior year in high school.

West Point

- **Location:** West Point, New York
- **Nomination Requirement:** From a member of Congress
- **Service Requirement:** 5 years in the Army; 3 years in the Reserves
- **Athletics:** NCAA Division I Patriot League

MILITARY COLLEGES

Where Military Training Takes On Special Significance

In the United States, a Senior Military College (SMC) is one of six schools that offer military Reserve Officers Training Corps (ROTC) programs and are specifically recognized under 10 USC 2111(a). Military schools are places where there are a Corps of Cadets and a variety of military experiences. Cadets have formation, perform physical training, and wear their uniforms. The six SMCs are:

- North Georgia College and State University; Dahlonega, Georgia
- Norwich University; Northfield, Vermont
- Texas A&M University; College Station, Texas
- The Citadel; Charleston, South Carolina
- Virginia Military Institute; Lexington, Virginia
- Virginia Polytechnic Institute and State University; Blacksburg, Virginia

In the United States, a Military Junior College (MJC) is a military-style junior college that allows cadets to become commissioned officers in one of the reserve components in two years, instead of the usual four, through the Early Commissioning Program. The students must still go on to complete a bachelor's degree before serving as regular officer on active duty. Begun in 1966, the Early Commissioning Program (ECP) plays a major role in officer production. In some years, ECP Officers have accounted for over 60% of all ROTC second oieutenants in the United States Army. The program is a major financial incentive for students who receive their commissions early and serve as officers while still attending college, gaining service time for promotions and retirement. In 1984, the California National Guard received 95% (74 of 78) of its ROTC lieutenants from the ECP program. The Army Reserve has had similar experiences. With the United States' involvement in continuing military action in Iraq and Afghanistan, the number of ECP slots is again being increased. The five MJCs are:

- Wentworth Military Academy, Lexington, Missouri
- Valley Forge Military Academy, Wayne, Pennsylvania
- Marion Military Institute, Marion, Alabama
- New Mexico Military Institute, Roswell, New Mexico

- Georgia Military College, Milledgeville, Georgia

Army Reserve Officers' Training Corps (ROTC)

Army ROTC is the primary source of college-trained officers for the Army. It is an elective curriculum offered at more than 700 colleges and universities nationwide. Army ROTC consists of two phases:

ARMY ROTC BASIC COURSE

The Basic Course takes place during your first two years in college as elective courses. It normally involves one elective class and lab each semester, along with the requisite physical training and field training exercises. You will learn basic military skills, the fundamentals of leadership, and start the groundwork toward becoming an Army leader. You can take Army ROTC Basic Courses without a military commitment.

Freshman Year: Preparing For Success as an Army Officer

Topics covered include:

- Introduction to Army Leadership
- Army Customs and Traditions
- Military Operations and Tactics
- Goal Setting and Accomplishment
- Health and Physical Fitness

Sophomore Year: The Role of an Officer

Topics covered include:

- Applied Leadership Theory
- Communications
- Principles of War
- Military Operations and Tactics

ARMY ROTC ADVANCED COURSE: GRADUATE COLLEGE WITH A DEGREE IN LEADERSHIP

The Advanced Course takes place during your last two years in college as elective courses. It normally includes one elective class and lab each semester, in addition to the requisite physical training and field training exercises. It also includes a summer leadership camp. You will learn advanced military tactics and gain experience in team organization, planning and decision-making. To benefit from the leadership training in the Advanced Course, all cadets must have completed either the Basic Course or have attended the Leader's Training Course. Entering the Advanced Course requires a commitment to serve as an Officer in the U.S. Army after you graduate.

Junior Year: Leading Small Tactical Units

Topics covered include:

- Command and Staff Functions
- Law of War
- Weapons
- Team Dynamics and Peer Leadership
- Military Operations and Tactics

Senior Year: Transition to Becoming an Officer

Topics covered include:

- Training the Force
- Military Justice
- Ethical Decision Making
- Personnel Management
- Cultural Awareness
- Post and Installation Support
- Military Operations and Tactics

College-bound high school students and students already attending a college or university may be eligible for merit-based Army ROTC scholarships worth up to $20,000 for tuition and a $4,000 living allowance for each school year. Scholarship students must meet minimum eligibility criteria and agree to accept a commission and serve in the Army on active duty or in a Reserve Component (U.S. Army Reserve or Army National Guard).

Officer Candidate School (OCS)

Officer Candidate School (OCS) is a 14-week course to train enlisted personnel, warrant officers, and civilians with a college degree to be Army officers. Enlisted soldiers and warrant officers must have ninety hours of college before applying for OCS. Civilian applicants must have a bachelor's degree. College seniors may apply if enrolled in a degree producing program at an accredited institution of postsecondary education.

Direct Appointment

The Army offers direct appointment opportunities for civilian degreed professionals in selected legal, medical, and ministerial career fields. Professional experience can even earn a direct commission officer a higher entry grade, if qualified.

Warrant Officers

An Army warrant officer is an officer appointed by warrant of the Secretary of the Army, based on a sound level of technical and tactical competence. The warrant officer is a highly specialized expert and trainer who gains progressive levels of expertise and leadership by operating, maintaining, administering, and managing the Army's equipment, support activities, or technical systems for an entire career. Becoming a warrant officer requires great skill in a specific occupational specialty. Army warrant officers must demonstrate leadership abilities and have the desire and dedication to perfect their technical proficiency through professional development, training, and education. Through schooling, experience, assignments and promotions, they are trained to perform effectively in the highest, most demanding positions within their career specialties. A local Army recruiter can provide up-to-date information about how to qualify to become a warrant officer.

OFFICER TRAINING

Newly commissioned officers attend an Officer Basic Course (OBC), which prepares them for their first assignment. OBC contains a mix of classroom education and physical training. Much of the time is devoted to practicing leadership skills in a work-like environment. During OBC, which lasts about four months, lieutenants also participate in a vigorous physical fitness program. OBC instruction is provided by the branch of the Army that utilizes an officer's specialty. For example, newly commissioned infantry officers attend OBC at the U.S. Army Infantry School at Fort Benning, Georgia.

Special skills that may be needed by new officers are developed at a functional training course. Pilots complete their flight training after OBC. Army infantry lieutenants may volunteer for airborne (parachute) or ranger training. Some infantry officers complete additional certification courses as Bradley fighting vehicle commanders if they are being assigned to units equipped with that vehicle. Army officers are also provided advanced training and refresher instruction to meet the needs of the Army or their next assignment. These courses usually are not more than six months in length. For example, Army supply officers can take advanced courses in materiel management, air delivery of cargo, and food services management. Specialized courses are available in every career area. At various points during a career as an Army officer, there are opportunities to participate in professional military education such as the Combined Arms and Services Staff School or the Command and General Staff College. These programs prepare officers for the increasing responsibilities associated with career advancement to the more senior grades in the Army. They are primarily the study of the command and staff knowledge required to be a professional officer at higher levels in the Army.

ADVANCEMENT

Most new Army officers begin their careers as second lieutenants. A few officers receive a direct appointment to a higher grade. There are established points (time-in-grade) at which time an officer is considered for promotion. Army officers are selected for advancement based on being qualified to meet the requirements of the Army. The Army promotion process is designed to ensure advancement of the best officers. This process also promotes career development and promotes officers with the greatest demonstrated potential. Promotion to the grade of first lieutenant usually occurs at two years of service. After an additional two years of service, the best qualified officers are promoted to Captain. After being in the Army a total of nine to eleven years, an officer becomes eligible for promotion to major. This and subsequent promotions are more competitive.

While all officers compete with each other for promotion, the Army recognizes a need to retain the right number of officers with the skills to meet Army requirements. A selection board evaluates the potential of all eligible officers and recommends the best qualified in each career area for promotion. There are provisions for early promotions of outstanding performers (limited to no more than 10 percent of promotions).

EDUCATION PROGRAMS

Advanced education is a goal for most Army officers. Some officers may be selected to pursue full-time studies toward a Master's or Doctorate degree through programs paid by the Army. Many officers pursue advanced education on their own time. Here are some of the programs offered by the Army for the advanced education of its officers:

Advanced Degree Program

The Army Educational Requirements System determines the Army's need for officers with advanced degrees. Selected officers are provided an opportunity to attend graduate school for up to three years in a discipline required by the Army. After completing their graduate studies, these officers are assigned to positions that utilize their education. These officers can also anticipate future assignments that capitalize on their specialized knowledge. Officers are considered for this program after completing six to eight years of active duty.

Fully Funded Legal Education Program (FLEP)

The Judge Advocate General's Funded Legal Education Program allows up to 25 officers to be selected each year to attend a regular course of instruction leading to a Juris Doctor (J.D.) or Bachelor of Law (LL.B.) degree at an approved civilian law school. These programs are provided at government expense and usually last three academic years. Upon completion, the officer is required to accept an appointment in the Judge Advocate General's Corps for the period of active duty obligation.

Training With Industry (TWI) Program

The TWI program provides training in industrial procedures and practices not available through military or civilian schools. It provides officers with vital knowledge, experience and perspective in management and operational techniques. This experience is necessary to fill positions of significant responsibility in Army commands and activities that normally deal with civilian industry. Currently, these programs are concentrated in the areas of artificial intelligence, aviation logistics, communications/electronics, finance, marketing, ordnance, physical security, procurement, public affairs, research and development, systems automation, and transportation. These programs normally last one year, with a predetermined follow-up assignment.

AFFIRMATIVE ACTION AND EQUAL OPPORTUNITY IN THE MILITARY

Concepts & Principles

Today's military leadership is fully committed to equal opportunity. This commitment has produced considerable progress, but more remains to be done, particularly for women. Historically, the Army has been the most successful of all the services at racial integration – a record, one official explained, built on "necessity, control and commitment." More specifically:

First, the current leadership views complete racial integration as a military necessity—that is, as a prerequisite to a cohesive, and therefore effective, fighting force. In short, success with the challenges of diversity is critical to national security. Experience during the 1960s and 1970s with racial conflict in the ranks was an effective lesson in the importance of inclusion and equal opportunity. As a senior Pentagon official said, "Doing affirmative action the right way is deadly serious for us—people's lives depend on it."

Second, doing it "the right way" means ensuring that people are qualified for their jobs; promotion is based on well-established performance criteria which are not abandoned in pursuit of affirmative action goals.

Third, the equal opportunity mission is aggressively integrated into the management systems—from intensive efforts at training to formal incorporation of EO performance into the appraisals used by promotion boards.

Fourth, the military has made very substantial efforts and investments in outreach, retention and training. These tools help build diverse pools of qualified individuals for assignment and promotion.

Fifth, despite the formality of the military system, the details vary somewhat across services. Different officials expressed slightly different perceptions about subtle aspects of how the system operates.[7]

The U.S. Commissioned Officer Corps

The commissioned officer corps is divided into ten pay grades (O-1 through O-10). Officers in pay grades O-1 through O-3 are considered company grade officers. In the Army, Marine Corps, and Air Force, these pay grades correspond to the ranks of second lieutenant (O-1), first lieutenant (O-2), and captain (O-3). In the Navy, these correspond to the ranks of ensign, lieutenant junior grade, and lieutenant. Officers in the next three pay grades (O-4 through O-6) are considered field grade officers. In the Army, Marine Corps, and Air Force, these pay grades correspond to the ranks of major (O-4), lieutenant colonel (O-5), and colonel (O-6). In the Navy, these ranks are lieutenant commander, commander, and captain. The highest four pay grades are reserved for general officers in the Army, Marine Corps, and Air Force, and flag officers in the Navy. The ranks associated with each pay grade are as follows: in the Army, Marine Corps, and Air Force, brigadier general (O-7), major general (O-8), lieutenant general (O-9), and general (O-10). In the Navy, they are rear admiral-lower half, rear admiral-upper half, vice admiral, and admiral.

COMPANY-GRADE OFFICER

SECOND LIEUTENANT (2LT) (Addressed as "Lieutenant")

Typically the entry-level rank for most Commissioned Officers. Leads platoon-size elements consisting of the platoon SGT and two or more squads (16 to 44 Soldiers).

FIRST LIEUTENANT (1LT) (Addressed as "Lieutenant")

A seasoned lieutenant with 18 to 24 months "time in service". Normally leads more specialized weapons platoons and indirect fire computation centers. As a senior lieutenant, they are often selected to be the Executive Officer of a company-sized unit (110 to 140 personnel).

CAPTAIN (CPT) (Addressed as "Captain")

Commands and controls company-sized units (62 to 190 Soldiers), together with a principal NCO assistant. Instructs skills at service schools and the United

States Army combat training centers and is often a Staff Officer at the battalion level.

FIELD-GRADE OFFICERS

MAJOR (MAJ) (Addressed as "Major")

Serves as primary Staff Officer for brigade and task force command regarding personnel, logistical and operational missions.

LIEUTENANT COLONEL (LTC) (Addressed as "Lieutenant Colonel " or "Colonel")

Typically commands battalion-sized units (300 to 1,000 Soldiers), with a CSM as principal NCO assistant. May also be selected for brigade and task force Executive Officer.

Flag-Level Officers

COLONEL (COL) (Addressed as "Colonel")

Typically commands brigade-sized units (3,000 to 5,000 Soldiers), with a CSM as principal NCO assistant. Also found as the chief of divisional-level staff agencies.

GENERALS

BRIGADIER GENERAL (BG) (Addressed as "General")

Serves as Deputy Commander to the commanding general for Army divisions. Assists in overseeing the staff's planning and coordination of a mission.

MAJOR GENERAL (MG) (Addressed as "General")

Typically commands division-sized units (10,000 to 15,000 Soldiers).

LIEUTENANT GENERAL (LTG) (Addressed as "General")

Typically commands corps-sized units (20,000 to 45,000 Soldiers).

GENERAL (GEN) (Addressed as "General")

The senior level of Commissioned Officer who typically has over thirty years of experience and service. Commands all operations that fall within their geographical area. The Chief of Staff of the Army is a four-star general.

GENERAL OF THE ARMY (GOA)

This is only used in time of war, where the Commanding Officer must be equal or of higher rank than those commanding armies from other nations. The last officers to hold this rank served during and immediately following WWII.

Part VIII
Advice for the Next Generation of U.S. Army Officers

No one wakes up and becomes a military officer overnight. It is a long and tedious process. Start preparing early. Stay focused and determined because there will be plenty of obstacles and distractions along the way. The following tips can help our next generations of leaders:

Elementary / Middle School

- Physical fitness: Obesity is a problem which is attacking our younger generation at an alarming rate. Become physically active at an early age and make it part of your daily life.
- Computer literacy: There is no avoiding this necessity. The earlier that a person is able to start learning basic computer skills, the better his or her chances are of succeeding.

Junior High School / High School

- Academic preparation (math, science, history and English)
- Requires a balanced blend of Academics and Athletics;
- Become fluent in at least one foreign language
- Volunteering, community service, church, self-discipline
- Become active in your high school Junior Reserve Officer Training Corps (JROTC).

Why Join Army Junior ROTC:

- To appreciate the ethical values and principles that support good citizenship.
- To develop leadership potential, while living and working cooperatively with others.

- To be able to think logically and to communicate effectively with others orally and in writing.
- To appreciate the importance of physical fitness in maintaining good health.
- To understand the importance of high school graduation for a successful future, and learn about college and other advanced educational and employment opportunities.
- To develop mental management abilities.
- To become familiar with military history as it relates to America's culture, and understand the history, purpose, and structure of military services.
- To develop the skills necessary to work effectively as a member of a team.

Advice for ROTC Cadets and Company Grade Officers

There is no one way to reach prosperity. What worked for one person may not work for the next. Each route to a balanced, prosperous life is just as unique as the person taking that journey. The truth of the matter is that prosperity comes from the inside, not the outside. It is more about having a balanced and centered life without losing control of what God has given you. You must keep it real. Do not forget where you came from as you climb that ladder of success. Keep in touch with your roots:

- Honor those who have contributed to your success (family, friends, co-workers, subordinates)
- Share your successes (family, friends, co-workers, subordinates)
- Remain humble, modest and grounded
- Be grateful for whatever success you obtain

Always remember and apply the basic leadership trilogy:

- Know your Stuff
- Take care of your people, and
- Be true to yourself.

Trust your subordinates, but verify their performance. Empower your subordinates, especially in front of their people. The corollary to this rule is to never tear your subordinates down in public. Never quit learning – no one is smart enough to completely master the environment for which he/she is responsible. If you think you know everything there is to know about a professional topic, you are likely to get a nasty surprise.

Be decisive and execute your plan aggressively. However, when conditions change unexpectedly, be flexible and adapt. Always have an alternative or tactical option. Don't forget to bring the rest of your team along as you change tactics. Sooner or later, you will find yourself working for a difficult superior. Never criticize that person to anyone. Always conduct yourself in a manner that shows the rest of team that you are loyal and backing up your superior. Your subordinates are always watching your every move.

Part IX
Reasons to Consider the Military Service

There are many reasons that each young adult should consider military service. While it is not for everyone, it is a viable and often successful option for many. Here are the three most important reasons any young adult should consider the military as an option after high school or college.

1) Maturity, Focus, and Pride

Every parent who has witnessed their child graduate from basic training will tell you how much they have 'grown up' in that short amount of time. Besides the growth in stamina and physical appearance, parents are often astounded by the self-esteem and self-confidence their young adult has gained. Your young adult will learn from the beginning to depend on himself and his unit for his very life. This teaches him how precious life is and how important and difficult it is to protect it.

Most important, he will learn that he is capable of doing the job. This insight gives a new soldier the maturity needed to protect our country. It impacts a focus of what life is all about. It gives him pride in himself and his country. Therefore, true confidence and self-esteem is gained.

2) Educational Benefits

The military will help pay for college and help pay off student loans. If your young adult is in need of money for education, the military is a viable option.

3) A Lifetime Career

Many people choose life in the military as their career path. They are successful in this chosen career, have families, and enjoy their lives. The military is not just a stepping stone to some other career; often it's a lifelong career choice.

BRANCHES OF THE U.S. ARMY

COMBAT ARMS BRANCHES

Infantry

- Encompasses positions concerned with the training and tactical employment of Infantry units, Infantry soldiers, and combined arms units.
- Evaluates intelligence, estimates situations, and formulates decisions.
- Coordinates employment of unit with other units.
- Commands attached elements.
- Directs communications, location and construction of Infantry positions and ground obstacles, and camouflaging of positions and equipment.
- Directs operation and employment of Infantry weapons and equipment such as rifles, machine guns, mortars, hand grenades, rocket launchers, recoilless rifles, armored personnel carriers and Bradley Infantry Fighting Vehicle.
- Directs training, administration, supply, maintenance, transportation and security activities of Infantry units.

Armor

- Encompasses leadership and staff positions concerned with the training and tactical employment of tank or armored reconnaissance units.
- Evaluates intelligence, estimates situations, formulates courses of action and makes decisions, coordinates employment of unit with other units (to include combat aviation).
- Commands attached elements.
- Directs communications, location and construction of positions, and camouflaging of positions and equipment.
- Directs operations and employment of tanks, armored vehicles, support infantry, and related equipment.
- Directs training, administration, supply maintenance, transportation, and security activities of the unit.

Field Artillery

- Encompasses positions that provide fire support to maneuver elements through the tactical and operational employment of field artillery systems.
- Commands, directs, and controls field artillery units at all levels.
- Directs technical fire control and firing operations using both manual and computer techniques. Coordinates the collective employment of joint and combined fire support assets to include non-lethal systems in support of the combined arms commander.
- Participates in the planning and development of doctrine, organization, training, material, leadership, and soldier initiatives to support the field artillery's role in combined arms operations.

Air Defense Artillery

- Responsible for the tactical employment, command and control, and the airspace management of both gun and missile units of Air Defense Artillery.
- Directs the technical and tactical operations, along with the engagement techniques used by various systems.
- Coordinates and provides the expertise at all levels of command, and develops the doctrine and plans essential to the successful use of Air Defense Artillery weapons in support of airland combat operations and defense against enemy aircraft and missile attacks.
- Develops organizational and operational concepts for future Air Defense systems.
- Directs training, administration, communications, supply, maintenance, transportation and security activities of ADA units.

Aviation

- Encompasses operational flying and non-operational aviation positions (less those identified with AMEDD AOC 67J) concerned with the employment and support of Army aviation units and elements.
- Directs and coordinates the employment of Army aviation units in support of land combat operations.

- Provides the Army expertise at all levels of command to develop doctrine and plans essential to the successful employment of Army aviation systems.
- Directs training, safety, administration, communications, supply maintenance, transportation, and security activities of aviation units.

Special Forces

- The Special Forces Branch ensures competent and confident leaders to exploit the Army's Airland Battle doctrine across the entire spectrum of conflict at all levels of warfare in joint and combined campaigns as part of the Army's balanced forces.
- Special Forces includes positions concerned with the employment of highly specialized Army units and elements to accomplish specific missions throughout the levels of warfare (Strategic, Operational and Tactical).
- Units are designed to operate with Airland Battle in the Deep, Close, or Rear areas of the battlefield to conduct unilateral operations or support the commander in his operational planning. Level of employment for Special Forces goes from low- to high-intensity conflict, focusing efforts to accomplish uniquely specific missions as the situation dictates in both developed and underdeveloped theatres of operation.
- Comprised of highly trained volunteers, each with extensive training in his specialty.

Corps of Engineers

- Combat Arms Branch that also has combat support and combat service support roles.
- Missions encompass military and civil engineering and the related planning, organization, training, operation, and development.
- Engineer officers are responsible for training and leading troops in combat, topographic, and construction engineering operations; facilities maintenance; civil works programs; and leading Engineer troops in infantry combat operations.

COMBAT SUPPORT BRANCHES

Signal Corps

- Manages Department of the Army and designated Department of Defense Signal assets, which include all aspects of automation and communications-electronics related to the planning, design, engineering, operations, logistical support and evaluation of systems and networks.
- Directs and manages the installation, operation, networking and maintenance of signal equipment.
- Advises commanders, directors, and staffs on command and control signal requirements, capabilities, and operations to include computers.
- Develops requirements for the design and implementation of data communications systems and networks.
- Establishes, prepares, coordinates and directs programs, projects and activities engaged in unit level supply, maintenance, and life-cycle management of signal materiel.
- Directs and controls units and activities involved with the application of electrical, electronics, and systems engineering and management principles, in the design, test acceptance, installation, operation, and maintenance of Signal systems, equipment, networks, and facilities.

Military Police Corps

- Commands, directs, and controls military police and criminal investigation units in both the tactical and peacetime environment.
- Supports the tactical commander as the primary combat force to detect level-two threats in the conduct of the rear battle.
- Provides battlefield nuclear weapon security, tactical security, circulation control, and the detaining and or evacuation of enemy prisoners of war and civilian internees.
- Supports the commander in anti/countering terrorism; the enforcement of military laws and regulations; keeping of order; prevention and investigation of crime, apprehension and disposition of mili-

tary offenders; traffic and movement control; physical security of critical equipment, facilities, lines of communication, and the safety of Government officials.

- Directs or supervises administration of custody, control, care and rehabilitation of military prisoners.
- Plans, coordinates and directs criminal investigations, crime surveys, protective service missions, polygraph support and criminal investigation activities.
- Prepares plans, policies and regulations pertaining to organization, training, operations, and equipment of military police units and personnel for both tactical and law enforcement operations.
- Directs training, administration, supply, maintenance, transportation, and security activities of a military police unit.

Military Intelligence Corps

- Provides the commander with all-source intelligence assessments and estimates at the tactical, operational, and strategic levels dealing with enemy capabilities, intentions, vulnerabilities, effects of terrain and weather on operations, and predicts enemy courses of action.
- Directs tasking of intelligence collection assets.
- Produces threat estimates to support doctrine, training, and combat developments.
- Ensures proper dissemination of intelligence information and products.
- Manages interrogation operations of enemy prisoners of war and line crossers.
- Interprets imagery from overhead and other systems.
- Directs counterintelligence and operational security operations.
- Performs clandestine human intelligence operations and manages signals intelligence operations, including jamming and participating in performing deception operations.
- Manages these tasks at all echelons.

CIVIL AFFAIRS:

- Encompasses positions which require officers possessing specialized skills relating to the conduct and analysis of civil affairs operations and critical skills associated with politico-military awareness.
- Includes foreign language and cultural expertise which support national policies or implement national objectives across the conflict spectrum.
- Develops, plans, coordinates, commands, controls and evaluates strategic and tactical civil affairs operations policies, doctrine and activities for Army, Joint, and Combined civil affairs programs.
- Officers direct and participate in the conduct of civil affairs command support, foreign-internal defense, unconventional warfare, civil administration, and numerous other missions, both overt and covert, in peacetime or when activated for crisis or war.

Chemical

- Advises commander and staff on chemical and nuclear employment, defensive actions involving chemical, biological and radiological warfare, and plans for use of and defense against smoke and flame employment.
- Plans and recommends NBC training activities.
- Performs functions involving the life-cycle management of chemical munitions and materiel. Plans and directs the activities of chemical units.

COMBAT SERVICE SUPPORT BRANCHES

Adjutant General Corps

- Plans, develops and operates the Army's personnel, administrative, and community activities support systems to build and sustain combat readiness.
- Commands personnel and administrative units and serves as staff advisor in the design and operation of Personnel and Administrative (P&A) systems.

- Formulates doctrine and policy for, and manages, P&A systems for organizations and headquarters at all levels.
- Plans and develops refinements needed to assure that these systems meet present and future Army requirements, during both war and peace.
- Responsible for training programs in training centers, schools, and units for these systems.

Finance Corps

- Develops policies, coordinates, and performs all Army Finance and Accounting functions for organizations and headquarters at all levels.
- Examines, controls, and certifies military and civilian payrolls, travel, commercial accounts, nonapropriated funds, and other vouchers and claims.
- Directs disbursement, receipt, and deposit of public funds as an agent of the U.S. Treasury Department.
- Prepares, consolidates, and analyzes financial data and management information systems reports at all command levels in support of the Planning, Programing, Budgeting and Execution System (PPBES) process.
- Advises on nonappropriated fund matters.
- Provides administrative services in support of payment of legal obligations of the Army or collection of monies due the United States.
- Interprets financial laws and Comptroller General decisions.
- Plans, develops, and implements changes to finance and accounting systems which support the overall Army mission and takes advantage of advances in productivity and efficiency.
- Trains military and civilian personnel in all areas of financial management.
- Develops financial doctrine to support wartime missions.
- Commands various finance units.

Transportation Corps

- Manages all facets of transportation related to the planning, operation, coordination and evaluation of all methods of transportation including multi-modal systems.
- Commands all types of transportation, movement control and logistical organizations tasked with controlling and carrying out personnel, cargo movements, or logistics requirements within a geographic area.
- Recommends priorities, coordinates tasks, documents cargo and/or personnel to be transported, allocates resources, and determines mode(s) necessary for the optimum utilization of assets and timely mission accomplishment.
- Works closely with members of the sister services, and host country personnel, on all manners of transportation plans and operations to include logistical support.
- Possesses expert knowledge of commercial transportation industries and practices in order to provide timely and adequate support for military/Government requirements.
- Plays a key role in the research, development, procurement, and life-cycle management of transportation-related equipment and systems.
- Acts as a transportation instructor advisor, staff/exchange officer with U.S. Forces or allied nations.

Ordnance Corps

- Plans and directs the activities of Army units and organizations engaged in one or more of the following activities:

  - Materiel management and maintenance of armament, tank and ground mobility equipment, wheeled and general purpose vehicles, ground support materiel, and other mechanical equipment and associated non-mechanical equipment except for medical, aerial delivery, and cryptographic materiel.
  - Materiel management and maintenance of missile/electronic systems materiel including missile rounds and associated guidance

launching, handling and test equipment; command and control systems; directed energy systems; and logistics space systems; and test measurement, and diagnostic equipment (TMDE).
- Materiel management and maintenance of conventional and nuclear munitions and warheads, and associated maintenance, test and handling equipment.
- Detection, identification, rendering safe, recovery, or destruction of hazardous U.S. and foreign munitions.

- Advises the commander on logistical matters and the unit capability to perform its mission.
- Performs in a variety of positions related to materiel management involving activities such as organizational, direct, and general support maintenance, production control, calibration, repair parts supply, quality assurance/quality control (QA/QC), technical assistance, coordination, training and research and development.
- Responsible for logistical training in coordination with the S3 or G3.
- Maintains necessary liaison concerning logistical activities.

Quartermaster Corps

- Plans and directs the activities of Army units and organizations engaged in the acquisition, receipt, storage, preservation, and issue of equipment, repair parts, fortification/construction materiel, subsistence, petroleum products, water, and other general supplies (excluding ammunition, medical, and cryptographic materiel).
- Responsible for storage, maintenance, distribution, and disposal of air items, parachute packing, and preparation of cargo for aerial delivery.
- Coordinates and directs the collection of salvage, and/or abandoned property, unserviceable supplies and equipment and the disposition of such items through proper channels.
- Commands or directs units responsible for providing service support in the areas of laundry and shower, mortuary affairs, aerial delivery, Army Exchange operations, and the renovation of clothing and textiles.

- Manages subsistence, to include procurement, storage, issue, sales, accountability, preparation of subsistence supplies, and operation of commissary sales stores.
- Responsible for petroleum operations and management, to include procurement of petroleum products, determination of bulk and package petroleum requirements, storage, distribution and quality assurance.
- Makes recommendations on matters pertaining to supply and service support and other logistical matters.
- Establishes and maintains necessary supply discipline procedures to ensure the maximum utilization of available assets.
- Responsible for logistical training in coordination with the G3/S3.
- Primary planner for logistical support (supply and services) within the command.

SPECIAL BRANCHES

Judge Advocate General's Corps

- Manages delivery of total legal services to the Department of the Army and its members. Responsible for managing and assigning branch officers.
- Supervises training of personnel in legal functions.
- Develops and executes plans and programs in the fields of: criminal law and related military justice; administrative law; military personnel law; international, comparative and foreign law; claims; business, commercial and financial law; control, tax and property law; contract appeals; environmental law; regulatory law; intellectual property law; intelligence activities law; legal relating to military installations; labor and civilian personnel law; law assistance and preventive law; legislative relief; professional legal training; and medical jurisprudence.

Chaplain Corps

- Acts as staff officer for all matters in which religion impacts on command programs, personnel, policies and procedures.

- Coordinates/directs a complete program of religious ministries, including workshops, pastoral counseling, religious education, and other activities for active and retired military personnel and their family members.
- Duties include those which normally pertain to the duties of a clergy person as they may be prescribed by law and modified by the organizational mission and environment.
- Provides leadership for moral, ethical and human self-development programs.

Medical Corps

- One of the six officer branches of the Army Medical Department (AMEDD) and is a special branch of the Army.
- Composed exclusively of commissioned officers who have a degree of Doctor of Medicine from medical school or Doctor of Osteopathy from osteopathic school acceptable to HQDA. Encompasses those specialties filled by officers who are responsible for the professional care of the sick and injured.
- Maintain the health of the Army and conserve its fighting strength.
- Care is provided for the sick and injured in peacetime while, at the same time preparations are made for health support of the Army in time of war.

Veterinary Corps

- Consists exclusively of commissioned officers who are qualified doctors of veterinary medicine. Encompasses those positions filled by officers in which the knowledge and skills required and the services performed are associated with the health and welfare of animals, the prevention of human illness from food or animal sources, the wholesomeness and quality of subsistence and experimental and comparative biomedical research.
- Functional areas of military medicine are: food, hygiene, safety and quality assurance, animal medicine, (primarily of government-owned animals), biomedical and subsistence research and development,

prevention and control of animal disease of community health significance, preventive medicine, administration and teaching.

Dental Corps

- Special branch of the Army composed of commissioned officers who are graduates of a dental school accredited by the American Dental Association and acceptable to the Surgeon General. Officers must possess a DDS or DMD degree and a valid, current license from one of the fifty United States, a U.S. Territory, or the District of Columbia.
- Mission in peacetime is to ensure that each soldier is in optimal oral health and prepared to deploy without becoming a non-combat dental casualty.
- Secondary mission is to provide dental health care to family members and other eligible beneficiaries of the military community per Public Law.

In war, the mission of the Dental Corps is to conserve the fighting strength of soldiers by the restoration and preservation of oral health and function, and assisting in the emergency medical management of combat and noncombat casualties. In both peace and war, the Dental Corps has the mission to support casualty identification through dental forensic identification operations. The principal functions performed by military dentists are: clinical and laboratory dentistry, command and staff, teaching, and research. Teaching is identified as a separate function, although it is an-all pervasive element of the profession of dentistry and is implied in each of the functional areas.

Army Medical Specialists

- Special branch of the Army authorized by Section 3070 of Title 10 U.S. Code and is part of the Army Medical Department.
- Organized in four distinct sections: Occupational Therapy, Physical Therapy, Dietetics, and Physician Assistant.
- Composed exclusively of certified occupational therapists, licensed physical therapists, registered dieticians, and students in the U.S. Army-Baylor University Physical Therapy Program, the Dietetic

Internship Program, and the Occupational Therapy Internship Program.

These officers formulate policies and develop procedures for operation and improvement of their respective activities within fixed and field medical environments. They conduct and supervise the operation of these occupational therapy, physical therapy and dietetic programs and establish and execute quality assurance programs which ensure optimal standards are maintained. All three specialties assist the commander in implementing health promotion, wellness and readiness programs within the military community; participate in readiness and mobilization exercises, initiate and conduct field and clinical research and scientific studies; plan, direct and supervise educational and skill development programs for officers, enlisted personnel, civilian students and perform as staff officers within AMEDD and/or Army organizations.

Army Nurse Corps

- Provides the nursing care and services essential to the mission of the Army Medical Department. Responsible for all facets of nursing relating to the planning, management, operation, control, coordination and evaluation of all nursing practices.
- Responsible for the supervision, direction, education and training, evaluation and control of Army Nurse Corps officers, and civilian and enlisted personnel engaged in clinical nursing, nursing education, research and development, and administration.
- Makes recommendations concerning policies, programs and operations of health care activities.

Medical Service Corps

- Provides unique administrative, field medical, technical, scientific, and clinical services to the Army Medical Department and the Army.
- Assignments range from medical TDA and TOE units, to medical research, to serving as medical staff officers on major command staffs. Administrative duties include tactical and TDA hospital administration, patient administration, medical resource management, mental health, optometry and medical logistics.

The field medical responsibilities include patient evacuation, plans, operations and training, intelligence and serving as commanders and staff officers in various medical TOE units. The Medical Service Corps provides technical and scientific medical support that includes medical research, medical intelligence, pharmacological services, sanitary engineering, environmental health, and clinical and environmental laboratory services in fixed facilities and tactical units. Furthermore, Medical Service Corps officers provide clinical direct patient care services that include audiology, podiatry, mental health, and optometry.[8]

Part X
Closing Thoughts

We live in the land of opportunity. This is a nation of freedom, living under God, believing all citizens must have the opportunity to grow, create wealth, and build a better life for those who follow. Each generation has the opportunity to go farther than the previous one because it stands on the shoulders of that generation. The more we can learn from previous generations, the better our chances are at exceeding all expectations. For our next generation of leaders, it is important to realize that, despite all appearances to the contrary, you still have freedoms for which your ancestors labored and died to provide. The success of the next generation will require a consistent, total effort by the individual and his/her community (be it society, corporation, government and community). Prosperity is built upon progress, and progress is measured from the point at which we start. We may not always compete on an equal playing field. Acknowledge this fact and prepare for life accordingly. That preparation starts in elementary school, not high school. If you wait until high school to start preparing for life, you will find yourself already behind.

Part XI
My Outlook on the Future

Some people live an entire lifetime and wonder if they have made a difference in the world. My approach is to make a difference on a daily, weekly and monthly basis so that at the end, there shall be no doubt. Just because you retire doesn't mean you stopped loving what you do. I consider military retirement as a transition rather than an end. However, this transition gave me the opportunity to pause, reflect and reassess my life. That assessment is what leads me to the idea of writing this autobiography.

As I look into the future, there is so much that I want to do over the next 5-10 years. This includes re-establishing my marriage and re-connecting with my son. To be a better father, a man must realize that children need much more than monetary support. They need and deserve a father's love, time and attention. When children miss out on these essential things, they often exhibit behavioral problems such as uncontrolled aggression, defiance, apathy, and poor performance at school. I knew I need to become a bigger influence in Brandon's life and I needed to start now.

There are other things I want to accomplish over the next year or so, including:

- Write another book
- Start my own event promotion/engineer consulting business
- Continue to invest in real estate
- Start a family enrichment foundation
- Get more involved in my Church
- Get more involved in my local community

"IF I CAN DO IT, YOU CAN DO IT TOO.":
The Keys to success (from my perspective):

If I can successfully make it out of the 'hood and become a positive influence in society, then you can do it too.

"If you always put limits on everything you do, physical or anything else, it will spread into your work and into your life. There are no limits; there are only plateaus. And you must not stay there, you must go beyond them." —the great Bruce Lee.

1. First and foremost, put God first in your life.
2. Do not let past failures and present predicaments cause you to become disoriented or lost.
3. Success is not about achieving what someone else wants you to achieve. Success is about discovering your gift and using that gift to the best of your ability.
4. Get in the game! In order to win you must be an active participant in the game. Win, lose, or draw, do something. Don't just sit back and complain about the *rules of the game*, get out there and do something about it.
5. Aim for perfection; why not?

   "Aim for perfection, listen to my appeal, be of one mind, live in peace. And the God of love and peace will be with you." —2 Corinthians 13:11 (NIV)

6. Examine your circle of influence. I recognized the importance of creating a social environment that was conducive with where I wanted to go in life.
7. Much is required; so be careful what you ask God for and ensure that you are ready and able to handle what he gives you. *"To him to whom much is given..."* —Luke 12:48
8. Stay connected. Utilize your legacy to build a bridge to the future. Never lose touch with where you came from. We are not better than others because we moved out of the 'hood, got an education, and landed a good job. We are blessed and should be extremely thankful for everything that we have.

9. Make your haters and naysayers your footstools. Do all the good you can, in all the ways you can, for all the people you can, while you can.
10. Self-reliance/self-motivation. Expect no handouts.
12. Keep your nose clean and stay out of trouble. Security clearance/background checks are standard procedures for becoming an officer in the military. Should be almost flawless.

And when times get tough and you are considering quitting on your dreams, just remember these words from our Commander in Chief:

"Yes we can."
— Barack Obama, 44th President of the United States

Part XII
Acknowledgements

To God be the glory for the things that he has done.

FOR EVERYTHING YOU HAVE GIVEN ME

For all my friends who have always stood my my side,
For my parents under whose shelter I could always hide.
For brothers and sisters who looked after me lovingly.
For the love of my life for loving me so magically.
For the above and for the blessings that are many more,
I wish to thank you oh dear Lord to the very core.

Leroy Sharpe, Jr. expresses much love and a sincere thanks to:

- God, for being my strength. Without him, none of this would have been possible. I owe it all to him.
- My parents. God blessed me with two wonderful parents, and I will be forever grateful for how they raised me. They continue to inspire me, even after their death.
- My wife, Sonja, for being the backbone of our marriage and the source of my joy. Whatever I may have accomplished during my time in the military, I could not have done it without her.
- My sisters, Alveta and Michelle, and the rest of my family for so much love and support. Thanks for keeping me grounded.
- My son, Brandon, for helping me to realize the true meaning of manhood and fatherhood. God sent you here for a reason. You have unlimited potential. Pursue your dreams and do not let anything or anyone hold you back. I am so proud of you.

- Fraternity: My association with the Omega Psi Phi fraternity has taught me so much about life and being a just and well-rounded man. The lessons learned and connections obtained are truly priceless. Thanks for being the International Fraternity that you are!
- Friends: Friendship is something that is very special to me and something that I do not take lightly. I may know a lot of people but my circle of friends is fairly small. I can honestly say that my circle of friends is second to none. I owe each of you my sincere gratitude and appreciation for being there for me throughout the years (through the good and the bad).
- Coworkers: Thank you to the many officers, NCOs, soldiers and civilians whom I have had the distinct pleasure of working with over the past 23 years. So many memories. I will forever be grateful. Could not have done it without you.
- Mentors: I am truly blessed to have had some of the greatest mentors in the world. The knowledge, wisdom and advice they bestowed upon me are priceless. I cannot thank you all enough.

I can do all things through Christ, which strengthens me!

ENDNOTES

1. Michael L. Lanning, "The African-American Soldier: From Crispus Attucks to Colin Powell," pg 304.
2. Ibid, pg 405.
3. Patricia Romero, "Black Woman's Civil war Memoirs."
4. Ibid, pg 220.
5. "African Americans in the U. S. Army," http://www.history.army.mil/topics/afam/afam-usa.htm, Oct 31, 2011.
6. Marvin Fletcher, "America's First Black General: Benjamin O. Davis."
7. "Black Generals and Admirals in the Military," http://diversitygps.com/black-brass-black-generals-and-admirals-in-the-armed-forces-p191.
8. "Becoming an Army Officer," http://www.goarmy.com/careers_and_jobs/become_an_officer.html.
9. U.S. Army Branch Insignia, http://en.wikipedia.org/wiki/United_States_Army_branch_insignia.

BIBLIOGRAPHY

"African Americans in the U. S. Army," http://www.history.army.mil/topics/afam/afam-usa.htm, Oct 31, 2011.

Becoming an Officer. http://www.goarmy.com/careers-and-jobs/become-an-officer.html.

"Black Generals and Admirals in the Military," http://diversitygps.com/black-brass-black-generals-and-admirals-in-the-armed-forces.

Fletcher, Marvin E. America's First Black General: Benjamin O. Davis, Sr., 1880-1970. Lawrence, Kansas: University of Kansas, 1989.

Lanning, Michael L., "The African-American Soldier: From Crispus Attucks to Colin Powell."

MacGregor, Jr., Morris J. Integration of the Armed Forces, 1940-1965. http://www.history.army.mil/books/integration/IAF-FM.htm. May 2, 2001.

Romero, Patricia, ed. A Black Woman's Civil War Memoirs (Princeton: Markus Wiener Publishers, 1988).

U.S. Army Branch Insignia, http://en.wikipedia.org/wiki/United States Army branch insignia.